PRO TACTICS™

STEELHEAD & SALMON

PRO TACTICS™

STEELHEAD & SALMON

*Use the Secrets of the Pros to
Catch More and Bigger Fish*

W. H. "Chip" Gross

THE LYONS PRESS

Guilford, Connecticut

An imprint of The Globe Pequot Press

To buy books in quantity for corporate use
or incentives, call **(800) 962–0973**
or e-mail **premiums@GlobePequot.com.**

The Lyons Press is an imprint of The Globe Pequot Press.
Pro Tactics is a trademark of Morris Book Publishing, LLC.

Text design by Peter Holm (Sterling Hill Productions) and Libby Kingsbury

Library of Congress Cataloging-in-Publication data is available on file.

ISBN 978-1-59921-416-0

Printed in China

10 9 8 7 6 5 4 3 2 1

The author and The Globe Pequot Press assume no liability for accidents happening to, or injuries sustained by, readers who engage in the activities described in this book.

This book is dedicated to my two favorite fishing buddies:
my sons, Andrew and Peter Gross.
May we have many more fishing trips together . . .

CONTENTS

■ The father-son team of Jim and Colin McConville knows how to troll up Lake Erie steel. The average Lake Erie steelhead weighs 5 to 6 pounds. CHIP GROSS

The world of steelhead and salmon fishing is vast, and no one angler can ever hope to learn everything there is to know, even given a lifetime of fishing experiences. This book, rather than trying to cover all of the various techniques and equipment used across North America for those two species, will instead present various fishing vignettes—snapshots of experienced anglers from the Great Lakes to the Pacific Northwest to Alaska.

■ **Nate Shuman, owner of Tackle Haven in Benton Harbor, Michigan, hooks into a big Lake Michigan salmon.** CHIP GROSS

Various fishing guides, charter captains, private conservation organization professionals, outdoors writers, and just plain good fishermen have all been kind enough to share their hard-won fishing knowledge for this book, and for that I thank them. They've even revealed a secret or two. By reading their stories, you'll not only become a better steelhead and salmon fisherman, but you will also come to experience a little of the waters and regions they fish. My hope is that you'll be able to apply at least some of their tactics and techniques to the lakes, rivers, and streams you fish.

As you read this, I hope you're seated in a soft, comfortable chair, possibly before a softly burning fire, with something tasty to drink close at hand. So whenever you're ready, let's go fishing . . .

—W. H. "Chip" Gross
December 8, 2007

PRO TACTICS™

STEELHEAD & SALMON

STEELHEAD

■ This nice winter holdover buck fell for a $^1/_{64}$-ounce pink jig and tube tipped with a single salmon egg. This combination can be deadly during the winter season. COURTESY COREY BERGER ENTERPRISES

Powerful, beautiful, even graceful—especially airborne on the end of a fishing line—rainbow trout are one of the most sought-after of all North American freshwater game fish. Native to the Pacific Northwest and Alaska, rainbows have since been stocked into countless other cold-water lakes, rivers, and streams around the world.

But few people realize, including some anglers, that many of these same rainbow trout leave the streams where they were originally stocked or hatched and migrate to adjoining larger bodies of water, such as the Great Lakes or oceans. It is there, in these cooler waters filled with abundant prey fish, that the rainbows gradually lose their colorful hues, their bodies taking on the steely gray appearance that has earned them their famous name: steelhead.

Fish species, such as steelhead and salmon, that migrate from rivers and streams to lakes and oceans then back again are termed *anadromous* by fisheries biologists. Biologists believe that the steelhead's color change occurs because of the prey fish they consume while feeding in lakes or oceans. But that color change, like their migration, is only temporary, for when steelhead return to the natal rivers and streams from whence they swam, their full rainbow colors return in anticipation of spring spawning. Serious steelheaders believe there is no greater trophy fish in all of North America. If you're not yet hooked, you soon will be . . .

CHAPTER ONE

Steelheading Pacific Northwest Coastal Rivers

Terry Wiest

I started steelhead fishing at age thirteen," says Terry Wiest of Renton, Washington. "That first year I didn't even get a bite, but I was so fascinated by the entire experience that I knew that's what I wanted to do—someday become a proficient steelheader."

During Wiest's second year of steelheading he caught only one fish, but he

■ Steelhead can still be caught during the cold-water conditions of winter. It just takes fishing more thoroughly and deliberately, as steelies will be more lethargic. CHIP GROSS

■ **When stream fishing, don't forget a net. Many steelhead have been lost by anglers trying to land fish by hand.** CHIP GROSS

kept at it through high school, at times even skipping class to go fishing. "We lived right above Washington State's Cedar River, so I could fish anytime I wanted," he recalls. "And being on the river that much taught me a lot about steelhead, so much that I was able to gradually increase my catch rate. The challenge of steelhead fishing still excites me to this day . . . I just plain love it."

Unfortunately, Wiest no longer fishes the Cedar River, as the stream is now closed to steelhead fishing because stocks of fish have become reduced. "I still drive by the river occasionally and remember some of the holes I used to fish as a kid," Wiest says. "It's kind of sad to not be able to fish those places again."

But Wiest moved on to other streams, eventually achieving his childhood dream of becoming an expert steelheader. Today he is one of the most knowledgeable steelhead fishermen in the Pacific Northwest, and as head of Steelhead University, he shares his knowledge in both online and formal classroom settings. Steelhead University is a recent spin-off of the highly successful Salmon University, founded by charter captain Tom Nelson (see the appendix).

"In 2004 many people attending Salmon University started asking for similar fishing information and instruction about steelheading," says Wiest. "Looking back on it now, that makes sense, as most of the anglers who fish for salmon in the Pacific Northwest also fish for steel-

head. They usually fish salmon during the summer months and steelhead in the winter."

Wiest goes on to say that, by far, most of the steelhead fishing in the Pacific Northwest occurs in the region's rivers, not the ocean: "In the ocean, anglers target other salmonid species, especially kings and cohos. The reason is that steelhead have somewhat strange migration habits and patterns. For example, they migrate in the top 10 feet of the water column and tend to not do so in large schools, as do salmon. Steelhead are also more spread out, so are harder to find in any numbers. There are a few places, such as maybe a point along a lagoon, where steelhead can be caught from shore as they migrate through an area, but in general it's tough to find concentrations of them in salt water. It's not until steelhead get to the freshwater rivers that most fishermen begin to target them specifically."

Anglers fish for steelhead in Pacific Northwest coastal rivers of all sizes, from large to small. For instance, thousands of fish enter the Columbia River, which is huge, but most of them eventually end up branching off into smaller tributary streams to spawn. Wiest notes that "the majority of steelheaders fish in those smaller rivers—rivers where they can easily and safely use a drift boat, jet sled, or even fish from the bank."

Wiest does much of his steelheading from a 10-foot, white-water-style pontoon boat, a Skookum Steelheader. He uses it strictly for transporting himself downriver from hole to hole, not fishing. "I launch my pontoon where the drift boats and other boats launch and make the same drifts they do, but instead of casting from my boat, I pull over to shore, get out, and walk the river's edge, fishing the various holes from the bank. I believe that I can fish a hole more thoroughly that way." Wiest's pontoon boat is also light enough that if he encounters a particularly treacherous stretch of white water, he and a buddy sim-

ply carry the boat around the rapids, then continue fishing their way downriver.

Of the three general groups of steelhead anglers in the Pacific Northwest—fly fishermen, bait anglers, and lure anglers—fly fishermen are the smallest lot. "Probably at the most 5 percent of steelheaders in the region are fly fishermen," according to Wiest. The reason why fly anglers are so few, in Wiest's estimation, is that other steelheading methods are simply more productive.

▕▎ **Terry Wiest caught and released this 15-pound native steelhead from Washington's Skagit River using a ⅛-ounce pink and white double-beaded marabou jig under a float.** ROB ENDSLEY

"Some fly fishermen in our area catch only one or two steelhead per year," says Wiest. "Personally, I want to catch more fish than that, preferably multiple steelhead in a day, if possible. And to do that in our rivers, float fishing or bait fishing is far more productive than fly fishing."

Wiest is best known as a float-fishing expert, and he has spent a fishing lifetime perfecting the technique. "I place a single jig beneath a thin slip bobber and float the rig downstream with the current. The technique is simple, but how you put the rig together is critical."

He uses a ⅛-ounce beaded marabou jig—never tipped with any bait—and ties a ¼-ounce inline weight directly to the leader. The inline weight helps the jig drop into the strike zone faster than it would on its own. He usually makes the leader about 3 feet long, but will increase it to 4 feet when fishing deeper water. The slip bobber, made by Anglers Advantage Tackle, is ⅜ ounce and black on the bottom with a fluorescent-colored top, either chartreuse or orange. The entire sequence for the rig is: main line—bobber stop—bead—float—bead—Palomar knot—inline weight—improved clinch knot—leader—improved clinch knot—jig.

Anglers Advantage also manufactures the marabou jigs that Wiest fishes. He prefers that particular brand because the jigs are made with Owner hooks, which he says will not straighten out under the pressure of fighting a big, powerful steelhead. He does not have a favorite color

of jig, but says that about 70 percent of his jigs contain the color pink: "If my life depended on it, and I had to choose just one jig to catch a steelhead, it would be pink and white."

Wiest uses spinning gear for float fishing. He likes a G. Loomis rod, model 1262 (10 feet, 6 inches), rated for 6- to 10-pound-test line. His reel is a Shimano Stratic, model 2500, filled with 30-pound-test PowerPro line. "The heavy-pound-test main line that I use has nothing to do with the fighting strength of steelhead. I use it because 30-pound PowerPro has the same diameter as 8-pound mono. It's easy to cast, and when I'm bobber fishing I want a line that floats on the water. Braided line has a natural buoyancy, making it easier to mend your line during a drift." Another reason Wiest uses a heavy main line instead of lighter ones is that when fishing in cold weather, small lines are harder to thread through floats and beads and make knot tying more difficult.

For leader material, Wiest likes 6- to 12-pound-test Seaguar fluorocarbon. "I strongly believe in using fluorocarbon leaders for steelhead, especially in clear-water conditions. I experienced a tremendous increase in my rate of hookups after switching from monofilament leaders to fluorocarbon."

When searching for river steelhead, Wiest looks for what he calls "holding water." "Optimally, I'm looking for holes from 4 to 6 feet deep, but fish can also be found in water anywhere from 2 to 10

DOING YOUR HOMEWORK

If you're unfamiliar with a fishing area, pre-fishing homework is critical to steelheading success. First of all, review the local fishing regulations. What fishing license or stamps are required? Where and when may you legally fish? Are there hook limitations or fly-fishing-only areas? Is streamside private property open to the public, or will you need permission from the landowner(s) before fishing private land? Also, fish possession limits sometimes change from year to year and/or area to area, so unless you plan to release the steelhead you catch, always check to make sure how many fish may legally be kept and of what length.

Next, take a look at maps of the area you plan to fish. State, county, and regional maps, as well as river maps, are all readily available, and many can be downloaded free from the Internet. In addition, Internet sites such as Google Earth (www.GoogleEarth.com) can be invaluable when scouting a new fishing location. Web sites are a great source of fishing information in general. Post a question on a message board, and you'll likely soon receive accurate information in return that will help familiarize you with an area. Who knows? You might even be invited by a local angler to fish with him when you arrive. And don't forget contacting bait and tackle stores. These establishments have a vested interest in seeing you catch fish, so will give you the straight scoop.

Knowing water flow rates before traveling to a stream will save you both time and money. After all, with the high price of gasoline and less and less free time these days, who wants to make an unproductive fishing trip? United States Geological Survey (USGS) Web sites provide up-to-the-minute information detailing river conditions. Stream flow on these sites is measured in cubic feet of water per second. If you know the ideal flow range for a river you'd like to fish, a quick check of a USGS Web site will tell you whether that stream is fishable. If you don't know the ideal flow rate, local anglers or bait and tackle shops in the area should be able to fill you in.

The size of a watershed determines how fast a river or creek rises and falls. In general, the larger the watershed, the longer it will take that stream to rise, fall, and then clear. Something to keep in mind if you can't find fishable water in the main stem of streams is to look to the tributaries. And don't overlook extremely small tributaries—many very big steelhead have been caught from streams so small that you can literally jump across them.

Surrounding land use also determines how fast a stream clears after a rain or snowmelt. For instance, streams draining mainly forestland will clear sooner than rivers draining agricultural land. So depending upon where they are located, streams of similar size can clear at different rates. Some rivers might clear in hours, where others may take days or possibly a week or more to be fishable.

feet deep. The perfect hole should have bottom structure, preferably fist-sized to basketball-sized rocks, and a few large boulders. The boulders create an eddy behind them, a place where fish can get out of the stream's current and rest."

Wiest goes on to say that when float fishing such pools, he likes his jig to suspend about a foot above the bottom. "In other words, if a hole is 6 feet deep, I want my float 5 feet above my jig. If I don't know for sure how deep a hole is, I'll guess at the depth, set my bobber, and make a cast. If I hit bottom with the jig, I immediately reel in and move my bobber stop 1 foot lower,

then cast again. If I don't hit bottom that time, I'm probably in the steelhead strike zone. If I do hit bottom, I continue the process of moving my float shallower, a foot at a time, until the jig is suspending a foot off bottom."

When fishing a pool where he cannot actually see a steelhead, Wiest makes parallel drifts of his lure about every 2 feet. "I've watched steelhead in clear water, and if they don't take a bait that drifts into them, they'll usually only move about 2 feet to the left or right. That's why it's critical to make parallel drifts every 2 feet across a hole, so that you don't miss any fish." Wiest also

■ **Because most western North American steelhead rivers are larger than eastern rivers, more drift boats are used for fishing the West.** JOHN BEATH

says that steelhead will often move to the end of a hole if they continually have a bait drift into them that they don't want, "but they may eventually strike that same bait out of anger or frustration, just to get it out of their stretch of stream. So make sure you fish a stretch of stream thoroughly, and don't give up too soon."

If a hole is not conducive to float fishing, Wiest is not opposed to drift-fishing bait. To do so, he changes rods—switching to a G. Loomis model 1082—and matches it with a level-wind baitcasting reel. For bait, he likes cured salmon eggs but adds no chemicals to the bait during the curing process, preferring a natural cure instead, such as borax. He also adds some color, saying, "I want a pinkish-red egg when I'm finished."

Terry Wiest has come a long way as a steelheader. From those first days of fishing the Cedar River as a teenager to heading Steelhead University today, he has spent thousands of hours streamside, gathering his hard-won steelheading knowledge and honing his skills. But he admits that he has not done it alone: "To become a better steelheader, I first began reading lots of fishing books and magazine articles. I was also fortunate to meet several steelhead experts along the way and fish with them. I stored away the little secrets they each taught me, and it has all helped make me a better steelheader. I constantly strive to be in that elite 10 percent of fishermen who catch 90 percent of the steelhead. Anyone can do it. All it takes is a willingness to study, learn, and spend time on the river."

CHAPTER TWO

Steelheading Western Inland Rivers

Scott Stouder

Idaho field director for Trout Unlimited, Scott Stouder was raised in western Oregon near coastal rivers and says that steelhead fishing is something that has been in his blood all his life. "I grew up only about 50 yards from the Alsea River," he says, "and I can remember many mornings when my brother and I would go down to the river and catch steelhead for breakfast."

Stouder now lives near the Salmon River in Idaho, another popular steelhead-fishing stream. "The Snake River Basin is huge, and the Salmon and Clearwater Rivers are two of its main tributaries," he notes. "They drain the central-Idaho complex of wilderness areas and roadless areas, making up some of the most pristine steelhead habitat remaining in the Lower 48."

The difference between the Salmon River and the coastal rivers where Stouder fished as a kid is that the Salmon is about 500 miles from the ocean. Meanwhile, the river he was raised on is only about 60 miles long and flows directly into the Pacific. "Consequently, the steelhead in those two river systems are very different, but in other ways very similar," he says.

Stouder explains that all anadromous fish are somewhat unique to the streams in which they were hatched, having different genetics in order to survive in those particular rivers. As an example, he compares steelhead that migrate a short distance up coastal rivers with steelhead that migrate hundreds of miles to inland tributary rivers, noting, "You can understand why the two types of fish inhabiting those rivers would be different genetically."

The steelhead that Stouder and others are fishing for in the Salmon River have had to make the 500-mile migration to and from the ocean at least twice during their lives. They swim the route once going downstream as juveniles—likely their most perilous journey because of their small size—and again returning as adults. (For reference, the Salmon River is a tributary of the Snake River, which is a tributary of the Columbia River, which empties into the ocean.) "It's really an amazing journey," marvels Stouder, "and most fishermen don't stop to consider that. To me it's fascinating, because I've lived in both parts of that world."

■ Scott Stouder, Idaho field director for Trout Unlimited, and a wild Salmon River steelhead. ROGER PHILLIPS

But coastal or inland, Stouder admits that steelhead are still essentially steelhead, and fishing for them is similar no matter where you go: "Both types of fish prefer the same kinds of habitat and respond in similar ways to water temperature changes. They also will take the same kinds of lures, baits, and flies. The fishing techniques that I learned while growing up along the Oregon coast have easily transferred to the Salmon River in central Idaho."

Once young steelhead hatch, swim downstream, and arrive at the ocean, they spend from two to four years in the Pacific feeding and growing before returning to

their native river to spawn. But steelhead, unlike salmon, don't necessarily die after spawning. They may return to the ocean a second time and may even make the return trip upstream again.

To emphasize this point, Stouder cites the steelhead stocked into the Great Lakes: "Those fish may spawn four to six times before they die because of relatively short migration routes. The same thing happens with steelhead in the shorter coastal rivers of the Pacific Northwest. A lot more repeat spawners show up in those small rivers. But for steelhead headed farther inland—in some cases hundreds of miles—migrating

■ **A wild Salmon River steelhead.** ROGER PHILLIPS

once during a lifetime is about all most of those fish can physically take. In general, it's unusual for steelhead spawning a long way from the ocean to make the migration journey a second time."

Steelhead ascend the Salmon River into Idaho annually in two waves. Most of the steelhead that arrive first, known as "A-run" fish, are two years old and weigh an average of 6 pounds. The "B-run" fish follow about a month or so later, trophy steelhead that have been in the ocean three or four years and weigh anywhere from 16 to 24 pounds.

"A-run steelhead arrive in early October," says Stouder. "The remainder of the month through the end of November is a popular time to fish for them, especially for fly fishermen. B-run steelhead begin showing up a little later, usually November through December."

He goes on to say that during winter the rivers in his area do not freeze solid, but will ice over. What happens when the water gets cold is that steelhead seek out the deeper pools, becoming almost dormant. They can still be caught during the cold-water period of the year, especially during a warming trend, but generally steelheading in winter is tougher than at other times of the year. When the water begins to warm in spring, fish once again become more active.

"Spring is when many of the real trophy steelhead are caught from the Salmon," Stouder notes. "You're looking for fish that are not in as deep of water as they were during winter. Good steelhead

water in early fall and spring, especially when fly fishing, is usually only 3 to 4 feet deep. But you can sometimes catch fish from deeper water, too."

Given the right river conditions and optimum water temperature—usually somewhere around 50 degrees—fly fishing on the Salmon is usually better in autumn and again in spring. During winter, when steelhead are in deep water, it's harder to reach them with fly gear. It can be done with lead line and weighted flies, but an angler has to rig almost like a bait fisherman to get steelhead to bite.

Most of the anglers fly fishing the Salmon River for steelhead use 7- to 9-weight fly rods matched with 8- or 9-weight fly line and a 10- to 12-pound-test leader. A piece of equipment that is becoming very popular in the region with fly anglers is the Spey rod, a long fly rod made for two-handed casting.

"A regular 7- to 9-weight fly rod is only about 8½ to 10 feet long," Stouder explains. "By contrast, a Spey rod can be as much as 13 to 15 feet long. Most fly-rod manufacturers are building Spey rods now. They're a specialty rod made for big rivers, but are used for saltwater fly fishing, too."

The advantage of a Spey rod is that it allows an angler to fish and cast more efficiently. When fishing large rivers, for instance, a fly angler usually has to cast relatively long distances. To cast again, he must strip in most of his line, then make several false casts to get line back out. All

■ Angler Tom Cross proudly displays a beautiful steelhead.
CHIP GROSS

of that takes time—time in which the fly is not in the water potentially catching fish. With a Spey rod, you raise the tip of the rod, do a kind of combination figure eight/roll cast, and your fly is back on the water in seconds. Fifty to 60 feet of fly line can easily be cast with a Spey rod, but the technique does take some arm strength. After a day of fishing with a Spey rod, your arms will definitely feel it.

For steelhead flies on the Salmon River, Stouder suggests anything relatively large and silver and purple with a #2 hook. "Don't expect to use the same flies you use for trout fishing, such as an Elk Hair Caddis or an Adams," he warns. "Think big, because you'll be fishing for big, strong fish."

Fly anglers on the Salmon will also at times use trailers, such as a bead-head fly, to help the main fly sink. This technique works well if casting a floating fly line. When fishing from a drift boat, many fly fishermen have two or three rods rigged: one with a floating line and one with a sinking line, and possibly a Spey rod. In that way they can fish whatever water presents itself without taking time to re-rig.

"The main thing to remember about fly fishing for steelhead is that it's very gear-specific" says Stouder. "You have to have the right tackle to be successful. But given good stream conditions, fly fishing for steelhead is very effective. It's a real thrill to battle and land a steelhead on a fly rod."

Other anglers on the Salmon River fish with either baitcasting or spinning equip-ment. Some fishermen just simply use a baited hook with enough weight above it to keep the rig moving with the current, ticking bottom every once in a while. But you have to know the various depths in the river well to use this technique, as the rig can tend to snag often.

It's easier for most anglers to present bait below a float. The float does double duty, both holding the bait off the bottom and presenting it more vertically in the water column, an advantage over the bait moving at an angle through the current. For natural bait, most fishermen use either sand shrimp or salmon eggs, sometimes both. A 2/0 hook is a good choice when bait fishing. Anglers occasionally switch to a 1/0 hook, depending on whether mostly A-run or B-run steelhead are in the stream. Most serious bait fishermen use level-wind baitcasting reels matched with rods stout enough to handle a 20-pound steelhead.

If you enjoy casting lures with spinning tackle, crankbaits such as Storm Wiggle Warts or inline spinners are a good way to catch steelhead from the Salmon. In Stouder's opinion, "One of the most pro-ductive and fun ways to catch steelhead is with spinners in fast water." Eight- to 16-pound-test line, mainly monofilament, is used by spin fishermen. Some anglers like braid, but they will add a section of mono to the end of it. The mono leader helps absorb the shock of a steelhead hit, and will break more easily than braid should you get snagged, allowing you to retrieve the braided line.

■ **Holly Endersby holds a hatchery-raised steelhead caught from a drift boat along Idaho's Salmon River. Looking on is guide Gary Lane of Riggins, Idaho.** SCOTT STOUDER

Anglers both wade and use drift boats to fish the Salmon River. Stouder's favorite way to fish is to descend the stream in a drift boat, pulling over to shore occasionally to step out and work a stretch of river by wading. "You can also use a drift boat at tail-outs to actually sweep areas with a fly, just like you would if using a lure," he says. "A drift boat definitely increases your versatility, though you still have to fish the water thoroughly. You can't just float down the river and cast anywhere to catch steelhead."

Stouder explains that when fishing bait or lures from a drift boat, most anglers move their boat a little slower than the current, allowing the current to take the bait or lure downstream, in front of the boat. With the rods mounted in rod holders, the person controlling the drift boat works the baits or lures back and forth across the river. Most guides prefer fishing this way, because all their clients have to do is sit in the boat and watch the rod tips for a hit. There is usually a mark or two on the line, telling them how far to let the line out, usually 20 to 40 feet. Most drift boats fish two or three rods at a time, one on each side of the boat and possibly one in the middle.

The Salmon River—one of America's great steelhead streams—drains the largest portion of central Idaho; the Clearwater River drains the remainder. Both rivers

■ Art Talsma and a beautiful Clearwater River steelhead. Talsma always fishes either a green spinner or green fly on St. Patrick's Day. Looks like the strategy works. PHIL JAHN

This fat, prespawn female was taken float fishing with a spawn sack. When the fish are less active, floating the spawn sacks can be productive.
COURTESY COREY BERGER ENTERPRISES

are big, powerful water, at times 100 yards or more wide. Scott Stouder had this final thought about locating steelhead in such streams: "The real turbulent white water the steelhead won't use, but they will be in the seams close to it. Steelhead are like any other fish—they're found in transition zones. Much like land wildlife using edge habitat, steelhead like places where two or more habitat types come together. A seasoned steelheader can look at a river and tell where the fish will be laying. It just takes experience . . . time on the water."

John Beath

Another angler with thoughts on how to locate steelhead is John Beath, outdoors writer and communicator from Monroe, Washington. "You have to understand something about steelheading in the West," Beath says. "On the west side of the Continental Divide—it doesn't matter if it's California, Oregon, Washington, British Columbia, or Alaska—the fish in those rivers and streams are going to be living in colder waters, so are more lethargic. They're less likely to be extremely aggressive or as active as steelhead on the east side of the Divide."

The reason is that the west side of the Continental Divide has a colder, wetter climate, while the east side is more warm and arid. As a result, steelhead often stack up in certain areas of warm water at certain times of the year. One of those areas is Heller Bar on the Snake River, near the border of Washington, Idaho, and Oregon.

Beath recently fished that stretch with his father during the month of October, hooking twenty-four steelhead in a single day. "And in addition to all those steelhead, we had four doubles on at once and also released five chinook salmon," he says. "We certainly didn't land all the steelhead we hooked, maybe about half of them, but they were a lot of fun nonetheless. And any day spent on the water with your dad is a damn good day's fishing in anyone's book."

The steelhead that Beath and his father, Bill, caught on that autumn day ranged from 4 to 8 pounds. Using spinning gear (9½-foot G. Loomis rods, model 1141, with Daiwa reels, 10-pound-test line, and an 8-pound-test leader), they cast to seams in the current while side-slipping down the river in a 26-foot boat. Their guide, Greg Kain of Kain's Fishing Adventures, slowed the drift with a trolling motor.

For bait, the trio cast small globs of bright-red salmon eggs. Two #4 Gamakatsu hooks were used to hold the eggs, with a small corky tied between the hooks. The corky gives the rig both a little flotation

■ **These two river steelheaders have their options covered. Both are carrying fly rods, but the fisherman in the front is also prepared to drift bait or cast lures with spinning tackle.** CHIP GROSS

and some added color. To take the bait down in the strong river current and keep it bouncing along or near the bottom, the anglers used pencil weights.

"If you'd get a bait anywhere near those steelhead, they'd attack it," Beath continues. "They're very aggressive fish at that time of year, which is why you can hook so many during a day's fishing. They may not be huge steelhead, but by using light, sporty tackle, they're a lot of fun."

Snake River steelhead can also be caught on a fly rod. "From mid-September through October, it's a world-class steelhead fishery for a fly rodder," says guide Greg Kain. "You can expect to land three to five fish per day, sometimes more. The river is relatively easy to fish during that time of year, especially using a wet fly on floating line. When the water begins to cool in late October, it gets a little tougher for a fly rodder, so you may have to add a little weight in front of a fly at that time to get it down."

Some 300,000 steelhead return to the Heller Bar area every fall, 80 percent of which are hatchery fish, identified with a fin clip. Any wild fish caught by anglers must be released. If you don't have a boat, steelhead can still be caught from shore on the Snake River. "Anglers can fish from the beach or shoreline at Heller Bar and still catch steelhead," Kain says. "And the shoreline from Heller Bar all the way to Asotin is accessible by car on the Washington side of the river."

CHAPTER THREE

Steelheading Great Lakes Rivers

River anglers must make a choice regarding how to fish for steelhead. In general, steelheaders use three basic techniques: drifting bait under a float, casting lures, or casting artificial flies with a fly rod. The decision is largely determined by

▦ Jeff Liskay and a steelhead from northeast Ohio's Chagrin River. The fish was caught on a white spawn sack with chartreuse floaters, suspended under a float.
JOHN RHOADES

a combination of personal preference and river conditions.

Jeff Liskay

A fishing guide for more than two decades, Jeff Liskay of northeast Ohio pursues steelhead and salmon every month of the year, fishing waters in all of the Great Lakes states. He likes to keep his steelheading as simple as possible and describes the basic setup for presenting bait to steelhead in rivers and streams as a "modified panfish rig."

"Basically, it's just a typical crappie-fishing system: a float, split shot, and hook," says Liskay. "The critical difference is that with moving water in a stream, you have to keep the bait at the right depth, which for steelhead usually means somewhere near the bottom. That's where the know-how and experience come in."

To be effective in various river conditions, Liskay says that a steelhead angler needs three basic sizes of stick-type floats, each about 5 to 6 inches in length. A small float (about ½ inch in diameter at its widest point) should be used when fishing small creeks or low-water conditions; a medium-size float (about ¾ inch in diameter) is needed for average-flow conditions; and a larger float (about 1 inch in diameter) is used for high or muddy conditions. Liskay prefers Redwing Tackle floats, as that manufacturer offers a variety of lightweight clear-plastic stick floats. Good steelhead-specific floats are available from other tackle companies as well.

> ## WHAT'S A CENTER-PIN REEL?
>
> "Another kind of steelhead tackle that has become popular in the Great Lakes region in recent years is drift gear," says Bruce Dickerson, owner of Grand River Tackle in Fairport Harbor, Ohio. "And one of the newest additions is center-pin reels."
>
> The reel first appeared on the West Coast and moved to the Great Lakes through Canada. It looks something like a large fly-fishing reel, but has only two ball bearings and no drag system. The reel allows for long, drag-free drifts of bait in the river current.
>
> "Fishermen are matching center-pin reels with 11½- to 13-foot noodle rods," reports Dickerson. "And because the reel has no drag system, when you hook a steelhead, you play the fish by applying pressure to the edge of the reel with the palm of your hand."

A tip concerning floats: If the float you've already purchased did not come with a small piece of rubber attached at its base, add a small, thin piece of surgical tubing (which can be purchased from a bait and tackle shop or medical supply store) to the float. The tubing helps keep the float fixed in place and also cushions the monofilament line when the float is moved up and down.

Another tip is to apply lip balm (Chap-Stick, for instance) to the area on the line where your float will be sliding up and down. The lip balm acts like fly-line dressing, allowing the line to be picked up off the water easier when mending a cast. Liskay recommends mending a line three or four times during a drift: "Pick the slack line up off the surface of the water by raising your rod tip and stalling the float. That allows for a slower, more vertical presentation of the bait, and the drift becomes more natural."

Between the float and hook, usually about 3 feet from the end of the line, Liskay ties a #10 micro swivel. He then attaches enough weight under the float to achieve neutral buoyancy; in other words, the float is just barely remaining above the surface of the water. He likes to have enough of the float riding above the water so that it's easily visible, but at the same time he wants the fish to feel as little resistance as possible when picking up a bait.

As for determining how much line to have below the float, Liskay uses what he calls his 100 Percent Rule. "To get a natural presentation, I increase the length an additional 100 percent of the water depth I'm fishing," he explains. "For instance, if

■ Using the right combination of equipment is essential to being successful. Fast- to medium-action float rods combined with proper braided line and leader enable the angler to execute the perfect presentation of lure and bait. COURTESY COREY BERGER ENTERPRISES

I'm fishing in 3 feet of water, I'll start out with 6 feet of line between the float and hook. I sometimes get more snags fishing that way, but my presentation looks more natural to the fish."

Liskay weights his line with a couple of small split shot (BB size) about 18 inches from the hook. He uses non-winged split shot, believing it hangs up less than winged shot. The faster the current, the heavier the split shot needs to be and the closer it should be moved toward the hook. Several smaller pieces of shot are preferable to one or two larger pieces.

When drifting bait under a float, the size of the hook should be proportioned to the size of the bait. "A #10 hook is a good all-around size for river steelhead," says Liskay. Personally, he prefers the Daiichi 1150, an offset hook, because "it's flexible enough to bend out when I get snagged, but can be bent back without breaking and still catch fish." In clear-water conditions, Liskay sometimes uses a hook as small as #18 when presenting a single salmon egg. When the water is muddy, or when fishing a spawn sack with yarn, he might go as large as a #6 hook. "In general, carrying three sizes of hooks—#8, #10, and #12—in your fishing vest will cover most conditions," Liskay says.

Another productive steelheading technique, especially for beginners, is to fish a jig beneath a float. Specialty steelhead jigs are available, but any small jig with a fairly stout hook can be used to catch steelhead. To keep things simple, begin by purchasing just two colors: black and white. As for size, in extremely clear water $\frac{1}{80}$- or $\frac{1}{64}$-ounce jigs are not too small. In stained or muddy water, $\frac{1}{16}$ ounce is a better choice, as the bigger, bulkier presentation will help fish locate the bait easier.

"The great thing about fishing a jig is that it keeps the bait on or near the bottom of the stream, which is usually where it needs to be for catching steelhead," says Liskay. "That's why so many novice steelheaders can catch fish on a jig."

Liskay recommends tipping jigs with some type of bait, such as a spawn sack, mealworms, maggots, a live or salted minnow, or any of the Berkley products: Gulp!, Gulp! Alive!, or PowerBait. His favorite bait for winter steelhead is a 1-inch white Berkley Power Tube.

You don't need a fly rod to present artificial flies to steelhead—simply tie a fly on under a float as you would a hook. Egg-type flies work well, as do weighted fly patterns such as nymphs and streamers. Some of the more popular flies for steelhead include Woolly Buggers, Prince Nymphs, Egg-Sucking Leeches, stonefly and shiner patterns, and Clouser Minnows. A fly known as Sucker Spawn is also popular. If you're unfamiliar with it, the fly looks as if someone dropped a hook into a 1970s shag carpet and then yanked it out. For some reason, steelhead seem to love the pattern.

Liskay says that the secret to finding river steelhead is locating the turns and curves in streams: "Find those kinds of areas, and you'll find steelhead. What you're looking for are deep, quiet pools with gravel nearby. It's a lot like fishing for smallmouth bass. The section of river that has the most turns will usually be the section of river holding the most steelhead. It's that simple."

As Liskay points out, when the water is clear, steelhead will usually be found in the deepest, darkest holes they can find close to some kind of structure. But when water levels are high or on the rise, the fish often change locations, as they now have more current to deal with but more stream area available to them for escaping that current.

A great place to look for steelhead during high-water conditions is immediately downstream of any riverwide barrier, either natural or man-made. Dams, logjams, and other obstacles are all good places to fish. Steelhead moving upstream cannot swim past these obstacles and so will naturally congregate below them.

An island also attracts steelhead because of the gravel that is usually deposited along both sides. "In spring, if you find Canada geese nesting on a small island, you've likely found a good steelhead spawning location," Liskay notes. "Another great location in spring is to find the first spawning water—meaning gravel—near creek mouths."

Another consideration to take into account when deciding where in a stream to fish is angling pressure. If possible, stay away from other fishermen. Fishing for steelhead that have not been disturbed recently by other anglers is much more pro-

ductive than trying to catch fish that have been cast to repeatedly. And when looking for a place to fish, keep in mind stream etiquette. If another angler is already working a stretch of water, it is general courtesy to not crowd him or her. Move either upstream or downstream to the next pool. The Golden Rule applies here: "Do unto others . . ." You'll both enjoy the steelhead fishing experience more.

A final tip when deciding where to fish is to keep in mind streams that have not been stocked. That may seem counterintuitive, but some steelhead stray into rivers and streams where they were not planted or hatched. An added advantage is that these streams will usually not be fished as heavily, as many anglers won't know that steelhead are even present.

According to Liskay, water temperature is the key to deciding how to make your presentation for steelhead: "Forty degrees is the magic number. If water temperatures are below 40 degrees in a stream, steelhead are usually not very active. That means you should be using more natural baits or small, slow-moving artificials."

In general, the clearer the water, the more you want to use flies and smaller, natural-looking artificials. The more turbid the water, the more an angler should consider using bait, such as spawn sacks. But learn to be versatile, and don't leave a pool or stretch of river until you've tried several different techniques and approaches.

The best times during the day to go steelhead fishing in rivers vary by season.

In the fall, for instance, when the water is still relatively warm and steelhead are just entering streams, fishing is usually best early and late in the day. During winter, by contrast, midday is usually better, especially on a sunny day, as sun warming the water often triggers fish-feeding activity. Even a degree or two jump in water temperature during the winter can make a difference. In spring, as during fall, mornings and evenings once again become the preferred times to fish.

What time of year are steelhead easiest to catch in a river or creek? Here's the annual cycle: Fresh-run fish—those steelhead just entering streams from a lake or ocean in fall—are relatively easy to catch, as they are feeding heavily. Transitional fish—those that have been in the streams for a while and are beginning to "color up," or obtain the rainbow trout's traditional pink stripe down their sides—become a little tougher to fool. Once steelhead begin spawning, they have just one thing on their minds so are even more difficult to catch. (The peak of spawning in the Great Lakes region is late winter through early spring.) "Drop-back" steelhead, or "downstreamers," are those that have already spawned and are working their way back to a lake or ocean. As they do so, they use deeper holes and river structures, and as in fall are easier to catch because they are actively feeding once again.

For his steelheading equipment, Liskay prefers Fenwick rods. His two favorites include a 10-foot, 6-inch rod for drifting

SPAWN SACKS

Spawn sacks are nothing more than trout or salmon eggs tied together in a small mesh bag. A tip when fishing spawn sacks is to keep the size of hook in proportion to the size of bait. For example, in clear, low-water conditions, a spawn sack about the size of the diameter of a dime matched with a #12 hook is about right. In normal stream conditions, tie a spawn sack about the size of a nickel and use a #10 hook. In high, turbid conditions, a spawn sack the size of a quarter with a #8 hook is a good choice. And remember to hook the spawn sack so that it does not completely fill the gap of the hook. The gap should be exposed as much as possible for better hookups.

Small Styrofoam beads, or "floaters," can be added to a spawn sack to help keep it up off the bottom and avoid snags. Jeff Liskay adds two or three floaters to each sack he ties. His favorite colors for steelhead spawn sacks are pink mesh with chartreuse floaters, blue mesh with chartreuse floaters, white mesh with pink floaters, and white mesh with orange floaters. "Just remember that contrasting colors are the important thing," Liskay says.

bait under a float and an 8-foot, 3-inch rod for casting lures. Both rods are two-piece and matched with spinning reels. An

important consideration Liskay empha-
sizes for winter steelheading is to make
sure that any rod you buy has oversize line
guides, especially from the tip of the rod
down at least four guides. The larger size
will prevent the guides from filling with
ice too quickly in freezing weather.

As for fishing line, Liskay uses two
types: a stiffer, abrasion-resistant line and
a limp line, preferring monofilament for
both. He fishes Berkley Trilene XL in
10-pound test for cold-water conditions,
dropping down to 8-pound-test Berkley

Trilene XT for more abrasion resistance
in warmer water. He prefers Seaguar
fluorocarbon leaders, 3 feet long in 4- to
8-pound test.

Once you've carefully chosen your
river steelhead-fishing tackle, rigged it
properly, and decided where and when to
fish, the only thing left to do is make that
first cast. But as you're standing streamside, there are still a few things to keep
in mind. Jeff Liskay, for example, visually
grids off the hole he's fishing in his mind's
eye before he begins casting.

■ **Winter steelheading . . . are we having fun yet?** JEFF LISKAY

"If I'm fishing with a float, I know that where my float goes, my bait will go," he says. "If the water is 40 degrees or colder, my grids might only be 1 to 2 feet apart. And I might have to make multiple presentations on the exact same grid, meaning drift, to get a fish to bite. I also steer my float to the sweet spots in the river by over-casting, then retrieving the float and stalling it when I get it where I want it." Liskay adds that in water warmer than 40 degrees, drifts don't need to be nearly as precise, as fish are more active in warm water and more willing to chase baits farther distances.

Whether you're steelheading or fishing for any other finny species, when to move and change fishing locations is one of the toughest decisions in all of angling. It's a judgment call, but how do you know when to make that call?

A wise fisherman once said, "Never leave fish to find fish." In general, that's true, but there are exceptions to the rule. For instance, if you've worked over a pod of steelhead—possibly even caught one or more—in a particular pool or stretch of river and then you find that the fish are no longer interested, it might be time to move upstream or downstream and let the hole rest for an hour or so.

A good rule of thumb to help you decide when to change fishing locations is that the colder the water, the more slowly and deliberately you should fish. The reason is that steelhead, being cold-blooded, are by nature less active in colder water and sub-

STEELHEAD ALLEY

One of the best places to fish in the entire Great Lakes area is a region known as Steelhead Alley, which runs along the southern Lake Erie shore from northeast Ohio east through Pennsylvania into New York State. Steelhead Alley has the best steelhead catch rates in the Great Lakes, mainly because of intensive stocking efforts by state fishery agencies. (Ohio alone annually stocks 400,000 yearling steelhead into just five rivers.) For most beginning steelheaders across North America, one hookup per day is considered good fishing. Steelhead Alley can produce twenty or more hookups per day, equaling the steelheading in Alaska.

sequently need less food. That translates into them being more selective—some anglers might say downright picky—in what they eat during winter. "Discriminating" is a good description of steelhead feeding behavior in cold, clear water.

So how does an angler put that information to use? In general, when water temperature is below 40 degrees, fishing a large, deep river pool for an hour or more may not be too long. With water temps above 40 degrees, fifteen to twenty minutes is usually enough time to tell if steelhead are present, active, and willing to bite. Again, it's a judgment call, and the more experience you have fishing various river conditions, the more you'll know when it's time to go—or stay.

One last point about locating fish and knowing when to move: If you are doing most things right on a particular day on the river, you should see a pattern start to develop in three to four hours of fishing. Are steelhead on the gravel? Are they at the heads of pools? Are they in deep holes? Are they using tail-outs at the back ends of pools? Be observant, be attentive, learn to connect the dots, and you'll catch more steelhead.

Now on to lures. Three types of artificial lures usually suffice for catching river steelhead: spoons, inline spinners, and crankbaits. Liskay's largest steelhead of the year are usually caught on crankbaits, "and if steelhead hit a crank, they absolutely crush it."

In deeper water in and around river mouths, especially when casting from pier heads, Liskay uses Reef Runner Ripshads, Little Rippers, and Cicada blade baits. Upstream, in shallower water, he prefers a Luhr Jensen Kwikfish weighted with split shot. He casts the lure upstream and lets it descend with the current, working it in and around rocks and other structure. Productive crankbait colors for steelhead include silver-blue, silver-pink, and silver-chartreuse.

Casting spoons come in a variety of shapes and weights. In Liskay's opinion, the best all-around spoon for river fishing, especially from pier heads, is the Lit-

tle Cleo. The pear-shaped KO Wobbler can also be good, producing an attractive thumping that is irresistible to steelhead. Liskay also likes long, thin Krocodile spoons, as they can be cast a mile. Heavyweight Michigan Stingers are also productive from piers. Include at least some of the following colors when choosing steelhead spoons: silver-blue, silver-orange, gold-orange, and silver-chartreuse.

Among the easiest artificial baits for steelhead fishing are inline spinners—just cast 'em out and reel 'em in. Mepps, Blue Fox, Rooster Tails, and a variety of other brands all catch steelhead. A good selection in sizes from 2 to 4 should cover most river conditions. Remember to tie a good-quality ball-bearing snap swivel to the end of your line before attaching a spinner. A snap swivel accomplishes two tasks: it prevents line twist and makes for easy lure changes. As for spinner colors, chartreuse bodies are always a good bet, as are silver and gold blades. But don't be afraid to try darker colors as well, especially black bodies in clear water.

Fly fishing is another technique for catching steelhead in Great Lakes rivers, though not as popular as casting lures or drifting bait. The reason is that, generally, it's not as productive as the other two methods. There are times, however, when nothing will outfish a fly.

Most Great Lakes steelhead rivers are relatively shallow and small compared to the rivers of the West, so a 7- or 8-weight

■ **This giant buck came after a third drift over a classic wintering hole. It is very important to be patient and fish likely spots thoroughly. If you do not execute the perfect dead drift, you simply will not get a bite.** COURTESY COREY BERGER ENTERPRISES

fly rod is about right for steelhead fishing. And in most Great Lakes rivers, three fly-fishing methods are generally used.

The "Chuck-n-Duck" method involves attaching a fair amount of weight, usually split shot, on the leader at the end of a thin-diameter fly line. The weight actually helps cast the fly line, not just cause the tip to sink, so you're basically using a fly rod as a modified spinning rod. Tie a fly or two off the tippet, and you're in business. The Chuck-n-Duck is so named because of the split shot near the end of the line: If you're not careful while casting, you could crack yourself on the head a pretty good lick.

The second method of fly rod steelheading in Great Lakes rivers is the float method, and it has become increasingly popular in recent years. It involves using a floating fly line with a strike indicator added partway down the leader. Below the indicator, a couple of small, evenly spaced split shot are affixed, and at the terminal end, one or two flies. Casts are made upstream at a 45-degree angle, which gives the fly time to sink before reaching the intended strike zone. Mending your line during the drift will cause the fly—moving in the slower current near the bottom of the stream—to stay in line with the strike indictor, which is moving in the faster current on the surface.

Popular steelhead fly patterns for float fishing include Green Caddis Larvae or a Pheasant Tail Nymph, as well as egg patterns such as Glow Bugs, Oregon Cheese, and Clown Eggs. Typically, if an angler is fishing two flies at once, one will be an egg pattern and the other a nymph.

A third fly-fishing method uses a sinking fly line to cast streamer patterns. An 18-inch to 4-foot leader is usually tied, typically on the shorter side, along with a fly imitating a baitfish or sculpin, the size of which depends upon river conditions. There is some disagreement among fly anglers about using flies with weight, as sinking line alone will take the fly into the strike zone. Some anglers like the action of a weighted fly, while others insist the weight on the fly causes it to act unnaturally, therefore making it less effective.

"Steelhead will often aggressively attack such a fly, just like they would a crankbait cast on a spinning rod," says fly fisherman Andrew Gross of South Haven, Michigan. "The sink-tip method seems

■ It's a great day of fishing when you can bring home a beauty like this one. COURTESY COREY BERGER ENTERPRISES

to favor fish that are fresh to a stream—steelhead that are really aggressive. Once fish have been in the river for a while, the float method of fly fishing seems to work better."

The sink-tip method is also effective for "drop-backs," fish in the postspawn mode. Most steelhead go straight back to the lake to feed following spawning; however, some do remain in the rivers. If they stay, they are usually found in deeper downstream sections, away from shallow water associated with spawning gravel. These remaining fish feed aggressively.

Float fishing for steelhead with spinning gear can be as productive as using fly-fishing tackle, but both techniques have their advantages and disadvantages. "Spinning gear allows you to make longer casts with ease," Gross says, "but it's easier to control line with the longer fly rod. The fly line can be mended easier during a drift, keeping the fly in the strike zone longer."

CHAPTER FOUR

Trolling for Great Lakes Steelhead

Bob Hanko

"The most difficult part of trolling for Great Lakes steelhead is finding the fish in the first place, because they move so much," says Bob Hanko. A serious steelhead and walleye troller, Hanko owns Cranberry Creek Marina, located on the south shore of Lake Erie halfway between Huron and Vermilion, Ohio. "Steelhead can move 3, 4, even 5 miles in a day, always following the forage," Hanko continues. He suggests checking fishing Web sites, calling bait and tackle stores, and networking with other anglers to first find fish and then stay on steelhead from day to day.

■ Lake Erie troller and marina owner Bob Hanko nets a nice summer steelhead.
CHIP GROSS

According to Hanko, once a school of steelhead is located, the fish will usually be either in the thermocline (the layer of water that separates the warmer surface water from the colder, deeper water) or close to it, typically about half to two-thirds of the way down the water column. Some electronics are sensitive enough to actually show the thermocline as a wavy line on the screen. Hanko suggests running baits 3 to 5 feet above that line or where you're marking fish. "And keep in mind that steelhead will gladly swim up out of the thermocline to chase lures," he says. "I've seen them follow minnows all the way to the surface."

During one memorable fishing trip, Hanko noticed steelhead chasing bait so aggressively that shiner minnows were actually jumping out of the water. "When I saw that, I tripped two of the four Dipsy Divers we were pulling, allowing them to come up near the surface. As a result, we soon started catching steelhead," he smiled. "And the water was so clear that day you could see the fish closing on the baits. They looked like silver torpedoes attacking the spoons." Hanko's most productive method of trolling for steelhead is pulling spoons at about 3 miles per hour behind Luhr Jensen Dipsy Divers.

His favorite spoons for steelhead are Northern King and Silver Streak, about 4 to 5 inches in length. Steelhead are used to eating large prey, and it makes sense that steelies can see large spoons better than small ones, and from greater distances. As for spoon colors, Hanko prefers purple, orange, and black, or a mix of those colors on the same spoon. And in his opinion, all spoons should have silver backs, providing plenty of flash.

Hanko attaches his spoons to 6- to 8-foot leaders of 14-pound Spectra Power-Pro, a braided line. His main line is also PowerPro, but 50-pound test. In addition, he places an elastic snubber behind the Dipsy Diver to help absorb the shock of a steelhead strike. His rod and reel combinations are Daiwa line-counter reels on Daiwa Black Widow rods (8½ feet, medium-heavy action).

In addition to spoons, steelhead can be caught on crankbaits, especially when fish are high in the water column. Either flat-lining cranks or running them off planer boards is effective, as steelhead don't seem too concerned about the presence of a boat. Smithwick Rattlin' Rogues and Reef Runner

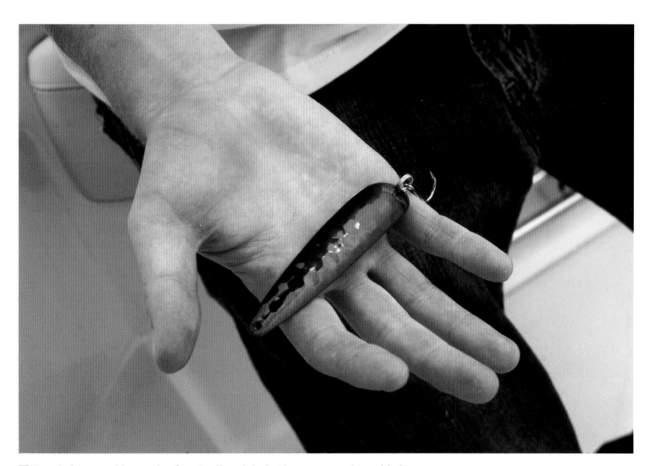

■ **Purple is a good lure color for steelhead, in both spoons and crankbaits.** CHIP GROSS

OHIO'S STEELHEAD STOCKING PROGRAM

Much of Lake Erie's excellent steelhead fishing is the result of an intensive stocking effort by the Ohio Department of Natural Resources (DNR). "Ohio annually stocks five streams with a total of 400,000 6- to 9-inch yearling Little Manistee River [Michigan] strain steelhead," said Ray Petering, head of the Ohio DNR, Division of Wildlife's fisheries section. "These fish migrate downstream into Lake Erie and spend two summers there, returning to the streams about eighteen months later." Steelhead caught by anglers in the Central Basin typically average 25 inches long and weigh 5 to 6 pounds. There is also a good number of fish over 30 inches and weighing more than 10 pounds.

Ohio's primary steelhead streams are the Vermilion, Rocky, Chagrin, and Grand Rivers and Conneaut Creek. Several other streams, including the Huron, Cuyahoga, and Ashtabula Rivers and French, Euclid, Arcola, and Cowles Creeks, get runs of stray steelhead. While the Ohio DNR has noted a small amount of natural reproduction, it varies greatly from year to year and is too low and erratic to support the quality fishery that has developed and anglers have grown to expect. Good quantities of cold springwater and adequate juvenile trout habitat are also rare in northeast Ohio's Lake Erie tributaries. The fantastic fishing—both in rivers and the lake—has been maintained not only by massive annual stockings, but also by many anglers practicing catch-and-release, especially in the rivers.

Rip Sticks are both good crankbait choices on the Great Lakes. Colors should be similar to the spoon colors already mentioned, again primarily purple, orange, and black.

The real fun of steelhead fishing is watching the acrobatics of the fish when they're first hooked. At times, they'll jump 5 feet or more out of the water. "They fight like no other fish I've ever caught," says Hanko. "It's really unbelievable. And once you get on an active school, it's sometimes difficult keeping two trolling rods in the water, let alone more."

Hanko goes on to say that steelhead fight so hard and are so acrobatic that you can expect to land only about a half to two-thirds of the fish hooked. They also have a hard jaw, making sharp hooks a must for good hook sets.

Lake Erie steelhead average about 6 pounds per fish, with an occasional 10- to 12-pounder coming aboard and an even larger trophy always a possibility. Early in the summer on Erie, steelies can be found anywhere from Huron, Ohio, north to Wheatley, Ontario, and then south again to Avon, Ohio. Later in the summer, the fish tend to move east of this triangle into the deeper, cooler waters of Lake Erie's Eastern Basin. An added bonus of trolling for steelhead far from shore on Lake Erie is the possibility of catching a truly trophy-size walleye of 10 pounds or larger.

As summer progresses into fall, steelhead start to stage at the mouths of Lake Erie tributary rivers in anticipation of their annual spawning run upstream. But before the fish make their move from the lake, anglers should try trolling spoons or crankbaits from diving planers or downriggers near the mouths of streams. Once the fish are in the tributaries, they are accessible to wading anglers all winter into spring.

In conclusion, Bob Hanko shares this final fishing tip: "I often find steelhead by first searching for a surface temperature break—a 2- to 5-degree difference—usually visible as a line on the surface where you see two shades of water coming together. Then I check my electronics to see what's under the boat, hopefully pods of baitfish with lots of steelhead feeding on them."

Captain Jim Cooper

Owner-operator of the charter boat *Limiter* out of Lorain, Ohio, Captain Jim Cooper

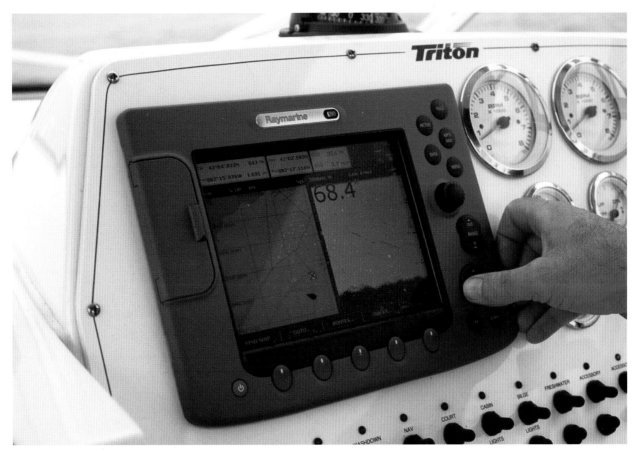

■ Dependable electronics are not only necessary for locating steelhead, salmon, and other offshore game fish in the Great Lakes, but often the GPS function is crucial for helping anglers find their way back to port. CHIP GROSS

■ Lake Erie charter captain Jim Cooper trolls for steelhead and walleyes by spreading lines horizontally behind his boat using a mast system with skis. CHIP GROSS is a retired police chief who now spends his time chasing steelhead and walleyes instead of bad guys. Fishing Lake Erie's Central Basin, Cooper has developed a solid reputation for consistently putting fish in the boat for his clients. And, unlike some captains, he is generous about sharing his hard-won fishing knowledge. Mainly a troller, Captain Jim runs as many as sixteen lines at a time, employing a combination of large planer boards (skis), diving devices, and downriggers to get his lures down and out from the boat.

"The first thing I do on any fishing day is check my sonar to see at what depth I'm marking fish," says Cooper. "It's then a simple matter of running lures at that depth. But simple doesn't necessarily mean easy. You have to not only figure out what type and color of lure to use, but also take into account wind, waves, current, line diameter, trolling speed, amount of line out, and other considerations.

"Take depth, for instance," Cooper continues. "How do you know for sure at what depth your lure is running? Most lure and diving-device manufacturers provide information on the depth their product will dive. These charts give a general idea of the depths baits run, but keep in

■ **An orange Dipsy Diver and spoon, a good combination for Great Lakes salmon or steelhead.** CHIP GROSS

■ **A combination of Dipsy Divers, Jet Divers, line-counter reels, and spoons are deadly for Great Lakes steelhead.** CHIP GROSS

mind these depths have been determined with a specific line diameter at a specific trolling speed. In other words, if they tested their product with 10-pound-test mono line at 1 mile per hour on a calm lake, and you're using 30-pound braid with 8-pound diameter and trolling at 2 miles per hour against waves, you can bet your bait is running at a different depth than is stated on the manufacturer's information sheet."

One of the ways Cooper suggests finding out for sure where a lure is running is to use a water-depth gauge. The gauge attaches to a diving device (such as a directional diver), and when trolled behind a boat at various distances and speeds, will record the depth it achieves. This is important information, because the depth a lure reaches is critical. For instance, if you're running baits below suspended fish, you probably won't get bit. Ideally, you want to be trolling lures at either the same depth as the steelhead you're marking on the sonar screen or slightly above. If Cooper is fishing spoons, he uses Luhr Jensen Dipsy Divers and Jet Divers to place those baits at the correct depths.

■ **Steelhead love spoons, such as this Michigan Stinger Scorpion. You usually want to "match the hatch" in size of spoon to size of baitfish, but don't be afraid to go a bit larger at times, as steelhead are voracious predators.** CHIP GROSS

Don't have a water-depth gauge? Here's an alternative: Run your boat at a known depth, say 20 feet. At trolling speed, put a lure or diving device in the water and begin letting out line. When the lure or device starts bumping bottom, you have determined both the speed and amount of line out needed to make that bait reach a depth of 20 feet. Continue this process at different depths with various lures and diving devices. The process is time-consuming, but you will eventually develop accurate information on how deep various baits run using your equipment.

How critical is trolling speed for steelhead? "Have you ever caught fish while trolling in one direction, but not been able to catch them in a different direction?" asks Cooper. "If so, that usually indicates there is current at the lure. There are several products on the market that will let you know what your speed is at the cannonball when trolling with downriggers. Two of the devices I'd recommend are manufactured by Fish Hawk and Sub Troll. These instruments also record water temperature."

As for steelhead lures, Cooper prefers spoons. "Steelhead like flashy spoons, such

■ Dipsy Divers can be adjusted in two ways. Tightening or loosening the tension screw (pictured) adjusts the amount of pressure required for the Dipsy to release when a steelhead strikes. Adjusting a weight on the bottom of the diving device determines how far the Dipsy will plane to the side of the boat. CHIP GROSS

as silver or other bright colors. An orange spoon seems to work well for me. I often catch steelhead while fishing for walleyes, but steelies usually like baits trolled a little faster. In spring, for example, I might be trolling for 'eyes at only 1 to 1.5 miles per hour, but by increasing my speed to 2 or even 3 miles per hour, I can often trigger steelhead to bite."

Cooper has not had much success catching walleyes consistently with downriggers, but steelhead are a different story. "With our relatively shallow water in Lake Erie, the cannonballs I run close to the boat

probably scare walleyes. But steelhead are curious, and not afraid of the boat or the cannonballs. I'll often run the downrigger just 20 feet down and catch steelhead. And when they hit a lure close to the boat, I'd strongly recommend having a loose drag setting on your reel."

Besides downriggers, Cooper catches steelhead on Dipsy Divers set on a number 1 setting just 20 to 30 feet behind the boat. "In clear water you can actually see steelhead hit the spoons on those lines closest to the boat," he says. "It's quite a thrill."

■ **Employing a mast system with skis helps trollers spread their lines behind a boat.** CHIP GROSS

In detail, here's how Cooper sets up his equipment in a typical steelhead-trolling spread: "Ohio law allows two rods per angler, so if I have six customers, a mate, and myself on board, I run sixteen lines at once, eight on each side of the boat. My spread normally consists of eight Dipsy Diver rods and eight planer-board rods, four each on both sides of the boat." He recommends using the same make and length of rod for all planer-board lines. He uses JBI 6-foot rods, fishing them off a mast system with skis, not inline boards. "And I stand the rods straight up in the rod holders," he continues. "That way, it's easy to tell if you have a small fish hanging on when you see one rod bent more than the others."

For his diver rods (JBI, Lake Erie Series), Cooper runs a combination of 6-, 7-, 8-, and 9-footers, giving him separation between rods when they're placed in a horizontal position in side-by-side rod holders. He uses either Okuma or Daiwa line-counter reels on all his rods.

As for line, Cooper prefers 50-pound-test braid with 12-pound diameter. And he recommends 25-pound fluorocarbon leaders, saying, "They're just about invisible in the water, soft yet tough, have minimal memory, are abrasion resistant, and have minimum stretch." He cuts his leaders in 6-foot lengths. He also believes that good-quality ball-bearing snap swivels are a must for attaching spoons to leaders.

For a final fishing tip, Cooper offers this bit of advice: "Controlling lure depth when trolling for any sport fish is extremely important. I'd rather be running the wrong lure at the right depth than the right lure at the wrong depth. It's also better to be running baits a little above fish than below."

But what if the steelheading is slow on any particular day? "I'm not afraid to experiment," says Cooper. "For example,

if I've trolled for a while and not caught anything, I let more line out on some baits to run them deeper and retrieve some line on other baits to run them shallower. I change lures and lure colors and vary my boat speed. I'll also change location if I have to, sometimes running several miles before putting my gear back in the water before setting up to troll again."

If all else fails, Cooper gets on the marine radio or his cell phone. "Other captains and I keep in touch and work together," he says. "If they're catching fish in a certain area and I'm not, they are quick to share that information. And I do the same for them. Everyone wins, because everyone ends up catching fish and the clients go home happy."

CHAPTER FIVE

Pier Fishing for Great Lakes Steelhead and Salmon

Most anglers don't own a boat, and if you find yourself in that situation, don't think you can't catch steelhead and salmon. Quality fishing can still be had by casting from shore at pier heads, breakwalls, or jetties. The secret is knowing the best times to go fishing, letting the steelhead and salmon come to you.

Just about every city and town, both large and small, along the Great Lakes' shorelines has one or more pier or breakwall extending into the lake. These structures

▓ **Fish on! Long rods are helpful for fighting fish as well as making long casts when salmon fishing from Great Lakes pier heads, breakwalls, and jetties.** CHIP GROSS

are usually open to anglers free of charge, and if a particular pier or breakwall parallels a river or creek, so much the better, as steelhead, salmon, and other species of fish will be attracted to the flow entering the lake.

"There are three main seasons for pier fishing in our area of southeast Lake Michigan," says local angler Andrew Gross of South Haven, Michigan. "As soon as the ice goes out in spring, most guys are fishing for Manistee-strain steelhead. Summer produces a Skamania run, a strain of steelhead originating in the Pacific Northwest transplanted to Lake Michigan. During fall is the traditional chinook, or king, salmon run."

Gross says that depending upon river conditions, usually about one quarter of the steelhead enter the streams in the fall. More trickle in during winter, but the bulk of the run is during late winter and early spring, April in particular. "If the ice goes out of the rivers in March, you can find fish staging near the pier heads, getting ready to make their runs upstream in April."

A bait that catches early-spring steelhead from ice-out through May anywhere in the Great Lakes is spawn sacks fished on or near the bottom. Eight- to 10-pound-test monofilament is usually sufficient as a main line. For weight, add a ½- to 2-ounce pyramid sinker that slides up and down the line. Most anglers then tie on a barrel swivel and 4 to 6 feet of fluorocarbon leader, usually in 8-pound test. The final

touch on the terminal end of the rig is a hook and spawn sack.

Adding a few floaters to each spawn sack helps keep the bait suspended just off bottom. The number of floaters added and length of leader will determine how far the spawn sack suspends. Some anglers tie a few spawn sacks with no floaters, preferring their bait on or within just an inch or two of bottom. Typically, spawn sacks for spring steelhead are tied smaller than for salmon, about the size of a nickel or dime. Four salmon eggs per spawn sack are about right.

"You might also catch a king salmon, coho, or brown trout during early spring," says Gross, "but in general, it's a steelhead fishery at that time of year." He goes on to say that beginning in late May and into June, Great Lakes pier anglers begin casting artificial lures, such as spoons, in addition to soaking bait. Half-ounce Little Cleos are a favorite spoon. The Cleos produce a strong thumping action when retrieved and can be cast a long distance.

As for crankbaits, Storm Hot 'N Tots are productive for pier steelhead. Chartreuse is always a good color choice, but if the fish aren't cooperating on any particular day, don't be afraid to experiment, not only with color but also with the crankbaits' size and action.

Though bait is the most popular option in March and April, some anglers fish spoons at ice-out. As the fish stage prior to their run, steelhead remain aggressive and, despite their growing urge to

■ Do glow spoons cast from Great Lakes pier heads just before dawn and again at dark really catch salmon? You bet! CHIP GROSS

spawn, will still be feeding. After the run, they make their way back to the lake, and if conditions remain favorable, will stay in shallow water.

Due to the energy spent spawning, steelhead feed very aggressively to gain back weight. Because some steelhead spawn early and leave the rivers while others are just arriving, it is possible in March, April, and May to catch one fish in prespawn mode and another indulging the postspawn feeding binge.

The second main season for Lake Michigan steelhead fishing from shore is during the summer, when the Skamania strain makes its move into the rivers. The run happens anytime June through August, and is dependent on the water temperature close to shore. "Some years the summer steelhead fishing is great in late June, but some years it doesn't really get going until late July," says Gross. "It's all dependent on when the lake turns over and the cold water from the middle of the lake moves close to shore. When it does, the Skamania follow it in."

For summer steelhead, anglers use the same bottom-fishing technique they did when fishing spawn, but replace the spawn sack with a whole shrimp. A floating jighead can be used to keep the shrimp off the bottom, and suspending a shrimp about 6 feet below a float can also be productive. Casting BJ spoons or KO Wobblers is a good tactic for summer steelheading from piers.

Both spring and summer steelhead prefer relatively shallow water, so locating your fishing position near the middle of a pier or closer to shore is usually better than fishing off the pier head. The opposite is true for fall salmon fishing. During autumn when casting to salmon, try to locate as far out on the pier as possible, casting into deeper water. And casting to the mud line—the line where river water meets and mixes with lake water—is also a good idea for fall kings. Keep in mind, too, that the fish will sometimes school, so if you find a hot spot on a pier, that location is usually worth fishing for several hours.

For Great Lakes pier steelhead and salmon, most anglers use longer rods—at least 10 feet—matched with spinning reels. This gear allows for long casts. The rods should be a medium action, as the increased bend helps cushion the long runs that steelhead and salmon are capable of making. Long, relatively soft rods are also more forgiving when fishing with lighter leaders.

A tip when fishing bait with spinning gear is to leave the bail open after a cast, placing a rubber band on the spool just in front of where the line comes off. Next, tuck a loop of line under the rubber band so that when a fish hits, it can take line but not feel any resistance. In essence, the spinning reel will be working like a bait-caster in free spool. Once you're sure that the fish has the bait, close the bail, reel down to take up line, and set the hook.

Here's another pier-fishing tip: Word spreads quickly during a strong steelhead or salmon run, and fishing pressure

When fishing from pier heads for salmon, try casting to the deepest water possible, usually off the end of the pier. For steelhead, try shallower water, along the sides of the pier and toward shore. CHIP GROSS

can get heavy; sometimes anglers will be standing shoulder to shoulder. As a result of seeing so many baits in the water, fish may become line shy. To counter this, use a light fluorocarbon leader, as light as you can get by with, possibly 8-pound test. Even smaller-test fluorocarbon will get you added bites, but it's a trade-off as to how many steelhead or salmon can be landed on the lighter line.

During the fall salmon season, most anglers are using a 12- to 14-pound-test main line, either monofilament or braid, and casting spoons. A white Little Cleo (¾

ounce) with orange spots has been a classic spoon bait from piers for years. But anglers will also mix it up during the course of the day and throughout the season, throwing a few crankbaits in addition to spoons. Storm Hot 'N Tots and Mag Warts—chartreuse, orange, or light blue—are productive, as they have a wide wobble and dig deep.

Fall pier fishing for king salmon on the Great Lakes can begin as early as mid-August and run through mid-October, with mid to late September usually being the peak of the run. Exactly when kings make their move into rivers is highly

■ **A combination of crankbaits and spoons will catch fall salmon when casting from piers, such as this jointed Rapala crankbait and Little Cleo spoon. Orange is always a good color choice.** CHIP GROSS

dependent upon rain and water temperatures. If the water in the rivers remains relatively warm and low, the fish will stay in the lakes, possibly well offshore. But several inches of cool rain over a period of a few days will often trigger salmon into the streams.

Keep in mind, too, that conditions can change quickly. With strong winds, for example, water temperatures at pier heads can drop significantly in as little as twelve hours. When that occurs, it's not just king salmon that are attracted to piers and breakwalls in the fall—steelhead, cohos,

lake trout, and brown trout can also be caught as bonus fish.

The hour right at sunrise often produces the best fishing for kings. Glow baits work well at that time, as well as just before sunset. As the season progresses, the first hour of daylight often becomes even more important. But if the fish aren't biting early, don't give up too soon. Depending upon water temperature and cloud cover, you can sometimes catch salmon throughout the day from piers.

Wind direction is always an important consideration. Most veteran pier anglers

■ A long-handled landing net is a necessity when pier fishing, as it can be a long reach from the top of the pier to the surface of the water. A wheeled cooler helps get fish and gear back home. CHIP GROSS

check the predicted wind and weather conditions before making a trip. If possible, you want to be fishing in the lee of the wind; in other words, have the wind at your back. Even a moderate wind blowing into your face can make pier fishing difficult, if not downright uncomfortable in cold weather. If bottom fishing, for example, waves crashing into a pier will tangle the leader and bait around your main line. If float fishing, wind and wave action will push a float into a pier, requiring almost constant casting to keep the bait where you want it.

Once a fish is hooked, the number one mistake most novice pier anglers make when first attempting to land a salmon or steelhead is trying to power, or "horse," the fish in. Even with heavier line, this is seldom a good idea. Set your reel drag loose, and let the fish run when it wants to. Hey, that's much of the fun of fishing anyway, right? And make sure you have plenty of line spooled. Salmon and steelhead are big, strong fish, capable of making long runs of several hundred feet or more. There's no worse feeling in fishing than to finally hook a nice fish, only to have it spool you and break off.

Many fish are also lost while attempting to net them. First, make sure that the fish is nearly exhausted before trying to net it. How do you know when the time is right? The fish will usually be on its side, gasping for air. Place the net in the water and lead the fish into it head first. Remember, you'll need a long-handled net to reach the water from most piers, possibly 10 feet or longer.

Once the fish is in the net, orient the net handle vertically, not horizontally, and pull the fish straight up. If you don't, you'll likely either bend the net handle or break it off completely. And before each fishing trip—or at least several times each season—check to make sure that the netting itself is not rotted or has holes in it. Most salmon and steelhead are large fish and their sheer weight can cause them to fall through a cheap or rotten net.

The Great Lakes: Last of the Midwest's Wild Places

An essay by W. H. "Chip" Gross

I was less than six years old and rubber-necking from the backseat of a 1950s Ford Fairlane. We were not a wealthy family, but my schoolteacher father had scraped together enough money to take my mother and me on a weeklong vacation. We were going to a cabin, and that cabin had a lake beside it—that much I knew. And I was going to get to go fishing—that much I counted on. Nearing our destination, my father remarked into the rearview mirror, "We should be able to see it soon . . ." And topping a rise, I caught my first glimpse.

On that perfect summer day a half century ago, the shimmering blue-green water before me shone as thousands of laser points. But it was not the sparkle that impressed me—I had seen light dance on water before—it was the sheer size of the lake itself, a vastness that I had no idea existed. Not only did water stretch as far as I could see from east to west, it also ran all the way to the northern horizon—and then disappeared!

That first glimpse of Lake Erie, my first of any of the Great Lakes, thrilled me

back then as it does yet today. Every time I first see big water, something in my gut twinges, tightens. I, like other anglers, am somehow inexplicably drawn to the Great Lakes. It's a combination of mystery (What lies beneath that vast surface?), danger (How many countless boats and ships have gone down and how many lives lost?), and angling adventure (How will the fishing be today?).

As fishermen, we know the Great Lakes are five beautiful, yet fickle, lovers. There are days when the fishing is almost too easy, and we are in love with each of these quintuplet beauties. Every bait, every lure tossed even casually over the side of the boat produces fish, and to top it off, a trophy or two comes aboard. But then there are those days when you do the very same things, fish the very same baits and lures in the very same ways, depths, and places, yet to no avail. The five lovers have become cold and standoffish. They've turned their backs. They've forgotten your name. There is no pleasing them . . .

After long hours of tough fishing on those lackluster days, your confidence

▇ **When salmon-trolling the Great Lakes during late summer or early fall, the first and last hour of daylight often produce the best fishing.** CHIP GROSS

finally gone, you slink from the water and tell no one at the dock of your catch. You wonder whether you've lost your touch. And on the drive home, after long periods of silence, and maybe to salve your bruised ego, you begin telling fishing stories of glory days gone by. But by that time the person sitting silently in the passenger seat next to you—the one who has possibly never fished the Great Lakes before until today, the one you bragged to so they would come along with you in the first place—is not buying it. He or she is sun- and windburned, hungry and tired, maybe a touch seasick, and in no mood for fish

stories. You know that person will likely never trust you again. Apologetically, you offer to buy a late supper.

But even though he or she may never return to the lakes again, you'll be back. There's no sure way to fully explain why, but you will. Though often mocked and made fun of by today's society as an anachronism, you're an angler. You've always been and always will be. You take quiet pride in knowing the ways of wind, weather, waves, and fish on big water. You know the primal feeling of being on the Great Lakes—adrift on the last great wilderness of the Midwest.

And a wilderness they are. Even though the lakes are surrounded by millions of people, we are only visitors upon their waters. When the lakes have had enough of us, they run us off for a few days—or a few weeks—with their gales. We have no choice in the matter but to leave, party crashers thrown out on our collective ears. For if we stay, there is literally hell to pay. Gordon Lightfoot said it best in his song "The Wreck of the Edmund Fitzgerald":

> Does anyone know where the love of
>   God goes,
> When the waves turn the minutes to
>   hours?

The *Edmund Fitzgerald* went down on Lake Superior, but it could have happened on any of the Great Lakes. They're all treacherous. Erie, for instance, being the shallowest and southernmost of the five, has more shipwrecks to its name than all the others combined.

As to size, the five Great Lakes hold one-fifth of all the fresh surface water in the world and nine-tenths of the United States' supply. These six quadrillion gallons of water, if spread over the Lower 48, would flood all of the land 9½ feet deep! The lakes are so large that the astronauts standing on the moon could see them. In fact, the Great Lakes are so well respected for their size and violence that they even merit a full page in Herman Melville's 1851 epic, *Moby Dick*, including such descriptive passages as:

> *For in their interflowing aggregate, those grand fresh-water seas of ours—Erie, and Ontario, and Huron, and Superior, and Michigan—possess an ocean-like expansiveness, with many of the ocean's noblest traits; with many of its rimmed varieties of races and of climes. . . . they are swept by Borean and dismasting blasts as direful as any that lash the salted wave; they know what shipwrecks are; for out of sight of land, however inland, they have drowned full many a midnight ship with all its shrieking crew.*

Finally, as an angler, you also know that the Great Lakes trade you fish for tackle and other equipment. They secretly keep track of the fish you extract from them and quietly add the subtotal to your tab. And just when you think you're ahead of the game, the bill comes due. I have personally lost a trolling motor, anchor, and countless lures, hooks, and lines to the lakes. Thankfully, I have yet to lose a boat, but I always get the feeling when on big water that I am but a flea on the back of some huge, living beast that could simply flick me off at its slightest whim. You've felt it, too. The water pulses beneath us, and we know that it lives. The waters of the Great Lakes call. And, as anglers, we must answer . . .

SALMON

■ Andrew Gross of South Haven, Michigan, with a chinook (king) salmon caught on a silver-and-aqua-colored spoon. CHIP GROSS

If you've never before stepped aboard a salmon-trolling boat, your first trip will likely be a fun yet bewildering day on the water. Because of the number of trolling tactics used, rods and reels seem to protrude from every possible part of the boat and at nearly as many angles.

Phrases such as "Set the diver back 100 feet on a number 3 setting" or "Fish on the 'rigger!" only add to the confusion and excitement. But as the day wears on and fish are fought, netted, and dropped into the boat's cooler—sometimes in staggering numbers and sizes—fishing techniques gradually become clearer. And by the end of the day, not only have the fish been hooked, you have too. A salmon-trolling trip to the Great Lakes, Pacific Northwest, or Alaska is one you will long remember— a memory you'll find yourself returning to again and again in your mind's eye.

In addition to trolling open water, salmon can be caught by "mooching"—the term for drifting bait in the ocean—or fishing tributary rivers. The spawning instinct of salmon is strong, and when the time is right, they cram into natal streams by the tens of thousands. Anglers then catch them from smaller boats, by wading, or even from shore. Salmon-fishing options, like the various salmon species themselves, are many. So are you a troller, moocher, or river angler? Whatever your preference, there's salmon waiting for you . . .

CHAPTER SIX

Salmon Fishing Great Lakes Rivers

Joe Cinelli

Joe Cinelli of Grand Island, New York, has been guiding salmon fishermen on the Niagara River for nearly a quarter century. Chinook salmon, as well as some cohos, migrate from Lake Ontario to ascend the Niagara each fall to spawn, and when they do, Cinelli and his clients are waiting for them.

"Jacks, one-year-old fish, usually weigh between 3 and 5 pounds," says Cinelli, "and fish between 5 and 9 pounds are two-year-olds. But the majority of the salmon returning to the Niagara River are mature three- and four-year-olds. Any fish over 22 pounds is definitely a four-year-old fish."

Cinelli adds that his clients catch primarily chinook salmon, the kings making up 99 percent of the fish netted from the river. "We do catch an occasional coho, but with the reduction in stocking of cohos by Canada and New York State, we see very few. But the second and third largest coho in the state did come from the Niagara River."

Cinelli's personal-best king salmon to date is a 37-pound male that measured 44 inches. But he says that as far as big fish are concerned, every year is a little different. "If there are good alewife and smelt populations in Lake Ontario in a given year, the salmon tend to grow larger. If not, well . . ."

In 2006, for example, Cinelli's clients averaged 22 pounds per salmon, but in 2007 the fish weighed only between 12 and 17 pounds. The largest salmon caught by a client in 2007 was a 24-pound female. Cinelli considers a trophy-size salmon out of the Niagara River to weigh anywhere from 27 to 35 pounds and measure 40 inches or more in length—a big fish in anyone's book.

To handle such large fish, Cinelli relies on Shimano tackle. He likes Convergence Series rods (7 feet, 6 inches) with a medium-heavy action, matched with Calcutta level-wind reels filled with 15-pound-test monofilament line, either Ande or Berkley Trilene XT. For terminal tackle, he first ties on a three-way swivel, then adds a 15-pound-test Seaguar fluorocarbon leader to the middle swivel. The leader measures from 6 to 7½ feet long. When fishing bait, such as salmon eggs,

■ Paul Liikala of Cuyahoga Falls, Ohio, hefts two nice Chinook salmon caught from New York's Niagara River during October. CHIP GROSS

he likes a Gamakatsu hook, the size (1, 2, or 1/0) determined by water clarity. His dropper line off the bottom of the three-way is between 4 and 8 inches long.

"If you make the dropper any longer, it tends to spin in the current and get twisted," Cinelli says. "And an added advantage of a short dropper is that it keeps your bait near bottom. The salmon in the Niagara are usually lying right on or near the bottom, so that's where your bait needs to be."

Cinelli goes on to say that while fishing the Niagara, you'll often see salmon porpoise, or jump, occasionally, but those fish are the exception. Most of the salmon that are feeding are along the bottom of the stream, and are caught by keeping the three-way weight bumping the bottom of the river, or at least within about a foot of it.

The sinkers that Cinelli uses are of a pencil-weight configuration. He uses a 1¾-ounce weight most of the time when the water is low, switching to a heavier weight—as much as 2½ ounces—if the river rises. (Throughout a day's fishing, the Niagara may rise as much as 4 to 7 feet.) The added weight also allows Cinelli and his clients to make as vertical a bait presentation as possible.

The main fishing technique that he and other guides use is to position their boat upstream from the salmon, then hold the nose of the boat in the strong current using a trolling motor. Most guides and other boat anglers on the river are running 18- to 20-foot aluminum deep Vs, outfitted with 150- to 200-horsepower four-

PREPARING SALMON EGGS FOR BAIT

Niagara River fishing guide Joe Cinelli prepares anywhere from 30 to 50 pounds of salmon eggs for bait each year in anticipation of the fall salmon run. Here's how he does it: "We remove the skein [egg sacks] from the salmon, slice them thin, then hang them up and let the water drain. We use a commercial salmon-egg cure or preservative called Pro-Cure, and brine the eggs in that solution for four to five hours. We also dye the eggs different colors, because some days salmon will hit light-colored eggs and some days they prefer dark-colored."

Cinelli then removes the salmon skein from the brine, laying it membrane side up on paper towels. He lets the eggs dry until they're tacky, and the membrane side until it feels like dried skin. He then places the eggs in plastic bags, adds borax, and shakes. The borax makes the eggs easier to handle and also helps to preserve them. The eggs are then frozen, ready for the following fishing season. A mature female king salmon can produce 7,000 to 10,000 eggs, weighing as much as 7 to 9 pounds.

stroke outboards. Once Cinelli maneuvers into position, he instructs his clients not to cast, but rather to lower their line over the side of the boat.

"What we're doing is essentially dropping our baits back to the salmon with the current," he says. "The first thing I want a fish to see is the bait hanging off the leader, not the dropper weight. For bait, we usually use anywhere from about seven to fourteen salmon eggs, attaching them with an egg loop just above a bare hook."

At times, Cinelli uses artificial lures off his three-way rig instead of bait. Luhr Jensen Kwikfish are a personal favorite. And because the river water has cleared so much in recent years due to the infestation of zebra mussels, natural colors of lures—silver-green, silver-blue, or solid silver—seem most productive.

Don't have a boat or the money to hire a guide? Good salmon fishing can still be had on the Niagara River from shore. Upon entering the river from Lake Ontario, salmon swim all the way to the base of Niagara Falls, but few anglers fish there because of limited access. Downstream from the falls the river roars through several Class V white-water rapids, then descends into a giant whirlpool. Many salmon congregate in that area, known as Whirlpool State Park, as do fishermen. But be prepared for a hike. The whirlpool is not accessible by boat, and you have to walk down some 246 steps from the top of the gorge to access the river.

Anglers fishing the state park use 7- to 9-foot rods rigged with 10- to 15-pound-test monofilament line. "We normally don't use braided line in the river," Cinelli says, "because if you get snagged, which can happen frequently, you'll probably lose all your terminal tackle. With the three-way swivel setup that I described earlier and monofilament line, if we get snagged we usually get the swivel, the main leader, and our hook or lure back." A tip here is to use a lighter line on the dropper weight than your main line. When fishing a three-way setup from shore, the rig is usually cast upstream, then allowed to bounce downstream with the current.

In addition to fishing with salmon eggs as bait, anglers at Whirlpool State Park catch salmon by casting inline spinners by day, such as a Super Vibrax #5, or Little Cleo glow spoons at night. "But I would not recommend that anyone fish the whirlpool area at night unless they have first fished it during daylight hours," Cinelli cautions. "It's just too dangerous." He pointed out that the river's water level drops at night, exposing rocks covered with moss and algae: "You'll be climbing over and standing on slippery rocks while casting. For your first trip at night, fish the whirlpool with someone who is experienced on the river."

Downstream from Whirlpool State Park is an area of the Niagara River known as Devil's Hole, the relatively small stretch that Cinelli fishes by boat with his clients. Pebbly Eddy, High Hole, Main Drift, Long Drift, and other well-known pools divide Devil's Hole into several sections. Depending upon the section, most of the water is between 17 and 22 feet deep, but

■ Occasionally charging a glow spoon with the flash of a disposable camera will keep it glowing underwater. CHIP GROSS

■ It doesn't always take a large boat to troll for Great Lakes salmon. A small inflatable will do the job if you stay in the tributary river mouths. CHIP GROSS

on some drifts anglers may be probing water as deep as 45 to 55 feet.

"The salmon fishery in the river has really changed over the past several years," remarks Cinelli. "For one thing, zebra mussels have cleared the water dramatically, altering the way we've had to fish. For example, back in the mid to late 1980s, it was relatively easy to catch salmon because the water was more tinged. You could fish the river with line as heavy as 20-pound test, use almost any color of salmon eggs, tie on a large 1/0 hook, and catch anywhere from fifteen to twenty kings in a single day's fishing. Today, because of the clear water, the fish have become a lot more finicky, requiring more finesse techniques. We now have to worry about egg color and the size of skein we're using as bait. We've gone from using golf ball–size globs of skein to pieces only about the size of a dime. The fish just don't seem to hit big chunks of bait anymore."

Later in the season as the salmon run winds down, steelhead enter the Niagara River. Cinelli adjusts by switching to a lighter rod and reel combination and downsizing to 10-pound-test line with 10-pound-test leaders, "but the equipment is still strong enough that I can land a salmon should I happen to hook one." He also points out that very few anglers use spinning gear on the Niagara, either for salmon or steelhead. "With a big fish pulling against both strong current and the reel drag, you can get a lot of line twist with a spinning reel. You don't get as much

twist with level-wind reels, and you also don't get as much line wear either."

When is the best time of year to fish the Niagara for kings? Traditionally, the three-week stretch from the last week of September to mid-October is the peak of the run. The main variable that might either accelerate or delay the run somewhat is water temperature. The very first fish of the season can arrive as early as late August. Early in the season, when salmon first enter the river, they're strong and ready to spawn. But after spawning, the fish begin turning brown in color and start to die, losing much of their great strength. So if you're looking for a battle, early season is likely better than late.

The New York State Department of Environmental Conservation (NYSDEC) stocks the Niagara River each May with thousands of salmon smolts, measuring 8 to 11 inches. In recent years the smolts have been placed in holding pens in the river for a few weeks prior to release. This "soft release" technique helps the young hatchery fish adjust to their new environment, resulting in increased survival and more fish returning to the river once they become mature.

In addition to instinctively wanting to return to the stream in which they were stocked, salmon and steelhead are attracted to the vast amount of water that the Niagara River pours into Lake Ontario—235,000 cubic feet per second. This massive flow is a huge draw for fish swimming anywhere near the river mouth,

■ **This is what most salmon trollers are after—big chinooks.** CHIP GROSS

even attracting salmon and steelhead that were stocked in rivers other than the Niagara.

An interesting final side note that anglers may not know about the Niagara River—but that affects fishing—is that the amount of water coming over Niagara Falls is intentionally reduced at night and during certain times of the year. The diverted water is used to generate hydro-electric power.

"The water flow changes after November 1 each year," says Cinelli. "After that date, the New York Power Authority and Ontario Power Generation are allowed to take more water from the river. But during the summer months, considered April 1 to November 1, they're required to let a certain amount of water over the falls during daylight hours for tourism purposes. How much water is diverted can really affect our fishing."

CHAPTER SEVEN

Trolling for Great Lakes Salmon

Surprisingly, salmon fishing on the Great Lakes is only about forty years old. It wasn't until the late 1960s and early 1970s that state fish and game agencies began stocking the lakes with five species of salmon and trout: chinook (king) salmon, steelhead (rainbow) trout, coho salmon, brown trout, and lake trout.

With an abundant supply of baitfish, mostly alewives, it didn't take long for the various species of salmon and trout to take hold and flourish—and anglers responded accordingly. By 1985 an estimated 3.766 million anglers were fishing for a combined 46.417 million days per year. And by the time the upward trend in angler participation peaked in 1989, the Great Lakes charter fishing fleet was up to about 3,000 boats, generating more than $35 million in annual revenue.

Captain Dave Engel

Someone who has observed many of these changes firsthand on the Great Lakes is Captain Dave Engel of Saugatuck, Michigan, one of the best charter captains and tournament anglers on Lake Michigan

today. Engel captains a 36-foot Tiara Yacht, named *Best Chance Too*, and has been fishing the lake since he was a teenager. He earned his captain's license at age eighteen and has been chartering ever since, some thirty years. During the past dozen or so years, Engel has also earned a reputation as a top-notch tournament angler, winning nearly a million dollars in salmon-fishing tournaments on the Great Lakes.

Engel begins his fishing year in early April near Michigan City, located on the very southern end of the lake. "There's warmer water down there because the lake is shallower and there are also steel plants and other warm-water discharges that attract fish," he explains. "When I'm catching thirty fish per day near Michigan City in the spring, other fishermen farther up the lake may only be catching three fish a day."

Engel says that the productive spring fishing in the southern part of the lake usually lasts a month or more. "April and May are always good. It's just a matter of whether you're catching all coho salmon, or coho and brown trout, or coho and kings. It's usually a mix of species." He adds that wind direction and wind velocity can either speed up the fishing or slow it down during the early season, depending upon the amount of cold water that blows into the area.

Engel's typical technique for fishing the southern end of the lake in early spring is to use crankbaits spread out behind the boat on inline planer boards. His favorite lure at that time of year is an orange Thin Fish crankbait, manufactured by Brad's Baits. At times, he also trolls either a Mylar or hair trolling fly, placing a red Luhr Jensen dodger (size 0/20) in front of it.

"When fishermen talk to one another over the marine radio, you'll hear the Thin Fish crankbaits referred to as either 'Old Gold' or 'Big Red,'" Engel says. "Original, jointed floating Rapalas are also good, as we're only fishing the top 3 feet of water in spring. The way we do it is to let a lure out about 75 to 100 feet behind the boat, then clip on a planer board. We run five or six of those setups per side of the boat, staggering them at different lengths out from the board."

As the water warms into May, Engel begins fishing farther north, along the

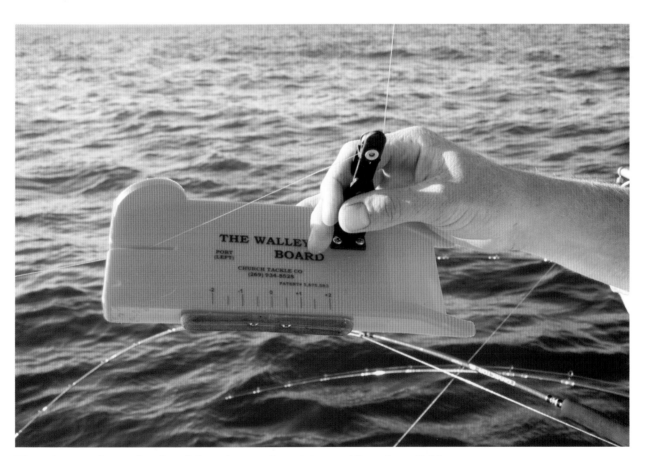

■ Just because it says "walleye" doesn't mean it can't be used for salmon fishing. Planer boards are used throughout the Great Lakes for spreading lines horizontally behind a boat when trolling. CHIP GROSS

east shore of the lake near St. Joseph, South Haven, and Grand Haven, Michigan. Typically, that area is the first place he begins catching good numbers of kings. "The month of May is always great on Lake Michigan," he says. "We often catch a limit of kings in an hour, usually three-year-old fish that weigh 5 to 7 pounds. Sometimes while pre-fishing for a tournament we may catch fifty or sixty of that size king—'cookie cutters' we call them—while we're looking for bigger fish."

Engel catches kings in May by pulling trolling flies behind rotators. "Length of the leader is the number one question asked by people attending my salmon seminars. I tell them that a good rule of thumb is to make the leader three times the length of the rotator. In other words, if your rotator is a foot long, the leader following it should be 3 feet long. The lure is then attached to the end of the leader with a quality snap swivel."

Engel goes on to explain the difference between a dodger and a flasher. Though at times similar in appearance, a flasher rotates a lure in a complete circle, 360 degrees. A dodger, by contrast, moves

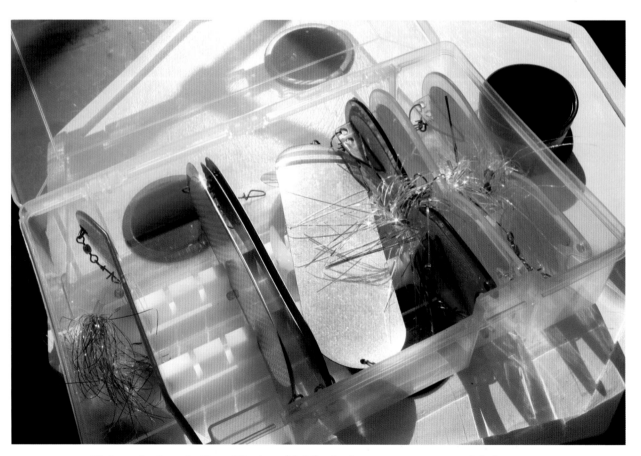

■ A good color selection of flashers (right), also known as rotators, and dodgers (left). Notice the trolling flies wrapped around the dodgers and flashers to save space when stored. CHIP GROSS

a lure back and forth in the water, but does not fully rotate. "Dodgers are extremely speed sensitive," he notes. "You have to troll slowly with dodgers, say 1.5 to 2 mph, to be most effective. The advantage of a flasher—also known as a rotator—is that they are not very speed sensitive. For kings, we fish with flashers in front of our lures as much as 80 percent of the time." Brand names of some of the more popular flashers on the Great Lakes include Spin Doctor, Coyote, and Smart Fish.

As summer comes on and the water continues to warm, June is usually Engel's most difficult month for catching salmon. The reason is that the water has not yet warmed enough to set up a thermocline (the layer of water that separates the warmer surface water from the colder, deeper water). As a result, fish are scattered throughout the water column as well as from the shoreline to the middle of the lake, making them difficult to locate.

"June is very unpredictable," says Engel. "You can have good fishing, but more times than not, June is everyone's toughest month. Fishermen in the northern part of the lake will usually do better than the southern end. August is usually the best summer month, especially in the northern half of the lake. Often in August you can catch a dozen or more fish before you get all your rods in the water."

Engel usually fishes near the Wisconsin shoreline in June, catching mostly coho salmon. As Lake Michigan waters warm, coho tend to migrate north up the

Wisconsin shoreline because of abundant baitfish and structure—underwater ledges—on that side of the lake. "During that time, pulling trolling flies behind dodgers is the most efficient way to catch coho salmon," he says. "I put a 1- or 2-ounce inline weight about 5 feet in front of a dodger, then attach an inline planer board. Typically, cohos are near the surface, but if they're deeper on a given day, I will also run spoons on downrigger lines or trolling flies behind rotators."

June and July also produce an offshore steelhead fishery on Lake Michigan. In-the-know anglers fish what's called the "scum line," a temperature break offshore. To explain, sunlight heating the lake causes water currents. Each year the southern, shallower end of the lake warms first, and that warm water moves north, up the shorelines. But Lake Michigan is so big that there is always cold water in the middle of the lake, even in summer. The slightest winds push that cold water into the southern end of the lake from time to time, and the fish follow it. These temperature differences are known as "breaks."

"To catch steelhead in summer, we do what we did for cohos just a month or so earlier," says Engel. "We pull Dream Weaver spoons in an Orange Crush color with silver or gold backs, and we do it near the surface behind planer boards in the breaks. At that time of year, if a spoon has any orange on it at all, it's a good spoon to use for offshore steelhead. The fish are usually in the top 20 feet of the

■ **A great day trolling Lake Michigan for king salmon! The three anglers holding fish are (left to right): Captain Bill Bale, Eric Guider of Shimano, and Captain Dave Engel.** TOM GREENBERG

water column, eating insects off or near the surface."

Catching king salmon is what Engel concentrates on the remainder of the summer, usually in the northern half of the lake. He does so by employing a combination of trolling techniques: copper line and inline planer boards, stainless-steel wire line and directional divers, and downriggers.

Engel notes that king salmon are extremely light sensitive, preferring relative darkness. They also prefer water temperatures in the low 40s to 60-degree range. "Depending upon water tempera-

ture, kings will typically be down 50 to 100 feet during summer, sometimes deeper. But by using the many different trolling techniques we do to get our lures deep, we can catch fish all day long."

During summer, he typically puts rotators (flashers) on every rod: 10-inchers on downrigger rods, 8-inchers on rods with stainless-steel wire line, and a mixture of both sizes on rods running copper line. "We're fishing mostly rotators and flies on our rods rigged with copper line," explains Engel. "We switched to copper line instead of lead-core several years ago, because we can use half as much copper line to achieve the same depth as when using twice as much lead-core. In other words, if it takes 100 feet of lead-core line to get to a certain depth, we can use only 50 feet of copper line to do the same thing. We're fishing more efficiently that way, catching fish faster with less reeling involved. And we can also control depth better with copper line. For instance, if we make a turn while trolling in relatively shallow water, we won't be snagging bottom quite as easily."

The copper line Engel uses is Howie brand, 45-pound test. He prefers Howie because, he says, the line has the most twists per inch of any copper fishing line on the market, giving it more weight. He does not segment the copper line, as when fishing lead-core. Rather, it's a continuous piece of copper with a fluorocarbon leader tied to the end. Engel uses 30-pound-test Gamma monofilament for backing his copper lines. He likes the fact that Gamma is abrasion resistant, has little stretch, and can be easily snapped in and out of releases.

"In addition to being more efficient with copper line, our customers can feel the fish better than with lead-core," Engel notes. "When a salmon shakes its head, you can feel everything that's happening down there on the end of the line. It's a lot more fun."

For leader material, he prefers 20-pound-test Gamma when fishing strictly spoons, 30-pound test when adding rotators in front of flies. He cuts his leaders in 30-foot lengths, replacing them when they get to be about 15 feet after tying and retying knots. Engel is sold on fluorocarbon for leaders because it has the same light properties as water, turning virtually invisible underwater. Fluorocarbon also has a certain stiffness that tends to give baits more action than softer monofilament leaders.

According to Engel, copper line has revolutionized salmon fishing on the Great Lakes. But fishing with copper line requires large-capacity reels with good drag systems. He uses Shimano Tekota 800 reels attached to Shimano Talora rods with stainless-steel guides, salmon-fishing equipment he helped develop. "If I'm fishing a tournament and it's a flat-calm day, and I need just a fish or two to finish out a limit, I may put out all copper lines with spoons," he says. "They're that productive."

In addition to rods and reels for fishing copper line, Engel also has rods rigged with stainless-steel wire line—seven-strand, 30-pound test. The stainless-steel wire lines are pulled down to the desired depth by directional divers, such as the Walker Deeper Diver. He usually runs one wire-line/diver rod on each side of the boat. One rod has a diver set on a number 3 setting, and the other rod is set at 1.5. At a number 3 setting, Engel knows that the diver is diving about 1 foot for every 3 feet of line out. At a 1.5 setting, divers dive about 1 foot for every 2 feet of line let out.

PRECISION ANGLING

If you're a troller, do you know the depth your favorite lures are running? Mark Romanack does—precisely. You see, Romanack is the author and one of the developers of the guidebooks *Precision Trolling* (now in its eighth edition); *Precision Trolling, Big Water Edition;* and *Precision Casting,* all three of which have become indispensable to serious Great Lakes anglers. And as helpful as the books are for both trollers and casters, the story behind their development is just as interesting.

The concept began nearly two decades ago when Dr. Steven Holt, a medical doctor, was fishing with guide Tom Irwin in Michigan. Holt was amazed that Irwin knew exactly how much line to let out to get his favorite lure to run at the proper trolling depth—knowledge that Irwin had accumulated through hard-won trial and error. After some brainstorming, the pair came to the conclusion that the process could be repeated for any lure and the information made available to other fishermen.

But Holt and Irwin had little idea how to market their new project, so they asked veteran outdoors communicator Mark Romanack for help. "I initially came on as a quarter partner in the company," says Romanack. "But eventually Tom wanted to sell his interest, so I owned half. And then a few years ago I bought the remainder from Steve, who still acts as a consultant to our company, Precision Angling Specialists."

The books are popular with anglers because each page contains a picture of a lure and the resulting dive curve for that particular bait with various lengths of line out. *Precision Trolling* includes data for about 350 lures, all crankbaits. *Precision Trolling, Big Water Edition,* has 150 dive curves and documents such devices as Dipsy Divers, Slide Divers, Jet Divers, Mini-Disks, and lead-core line. *Precision Casting* lists dive curves for about 140 crankbaits.

"The way we test the various lures is relatively simple, yet time-consuming," Romanack says. "At Higgins Lake in northern Michigan, a lake with clear water and calm bays, we suspend a line, marked in feet and inches, from a surface float. This 'story pole,' as I call it—nothing more than a tape measure, actually—is not anchored to the bottom. It must be free-floating so that it remains absolutely vertical in the water column. A scuba diver is then sent down to observe the lures as I troll them past the tape at 2.5 mph with various amounts of line out (using 10-pound-test monofilament), up to 250 feet. We feel very confident that we can measure dive curves to an accuracy of 4 inches."

Lead lengths are increased by 25 feet with each trolling pass, and the scuba diver surfaces after each pass to tell Romanack the depth at which the lure ran. Once a lure is tested at all lead lengths, the process is repeated to make sure that the data is accurate.

"We make at least two series of tests for each lure, and if the numbers don't match, we've made a mistake," continues Romanack. "If that happens, we repeat the process. It could take as little as an hour to test a single lure or several hours. It depends upon whether or not we have problems getting the bait tuned and running properly or any number of other variables. It seems that on some days Murphy's Law is definitely in full affect."

Romanack goes on to say that no two dive curves are exactly the same because of the physical differences in lures. "The buoyancy of a lure, its weight, the width and length of its bill, and the density of the plastic all determine how sharply and deeply a lure will dive. After all our years of testing, we have a pretty good idea how a new bait might run, but we don't know for sure until we actually get it into the water. Even lures that look similar don't necessarily run similar."

An added service that Romanack offers with his books is free technical support. "If someone buys a book and doesn't understand something or they have a question about a particular fishing situation not covered in the book, they can either call toll-free or e-mail me. I grew up in a family that was very business oriented, and I learned that personal customer service is what sets you apart. I get dozens of questions each day during the fishing season, and I always try and get back to fishermen in a timely manner with an answer."

Romanack also uses the information from angler phone calls and e-mails to decide what lures to test next. "It's totally customer driven. Lure companies do not determine what lures we test, anglers do. And because we're not connected with any manufacturer, our test results are totally unbiased."

In the future, Romanack will be working to get dive curves of new lures to the public faster. New editions of *Precision Trolling* are published about every two years, but he knows that many new lures come out in the interim and anglers want that data. "What we're thinking about doing is putting sample dive curves on our Web site prior to them being published in one of our books. An angler would then be able to look at the data, but not download it. But we're still not sure if that's the way we want to go. If anyone out there has a better idea, we'd like to hear about it. We're even considering creating an electronic version of our books that could be downloaded from the Internet."

If you don't yet have a copy of one or all three of these books, put them on your Christmas wish list—they're well worth the price.

"The advantage of directional divers is that they not only take lures away from the back of the boat, but they also move up and down in the water column as you speed up, slow down, and turn," Engel explains. "If I had to choose just one setup for kings, it would be a diver rod pulling a rotator and trolling fly. For some reason, a rod and reel loaded with stainless-steel wire line and fishing a fly behind a rotator and diver will catch king salmon all day long, while other equipment may or may not. I don't know why it works—possibly it's the vibration the wire line gives the lure. The most important thing is that it does. . . . That setup catches fish."

Engel also fishes downriggers as part of his repertoire. "First thing in the morning, downriggers are the quickest, most efficient way to catch king salmon. But when fishing 'riggers, you need some kind of device to monitor speed through the water and temperature at the downrigger ball. The best device I've found is the Fish Hawk. It's a wireless unit, sending an electronic pulse up to a transducer on the boat."

He runs three Vector downriggers, mounting one in the center of the transom, the other two about 5 feet up either side of the boat. Such a setup leaves the corners of the back of the boat open for landing fish. "We normally fish 20 to 40 feet deep with our downrigger rods, usually running spoons. I always put the center downrigger the deepest, with the side downriggers running shallower."

Engel also believes that a good downrigger release is what should actually hook a fish, not the fisherman. "If every time you get a bite the downrigger line pops out of the release on its own, your release is set too loose. That's the number one mistake most people make when fishing downriggers. A release should be set tight enough

so that you see the rod tip bouncing up and down when a fish hits."

He goes on to explain that the angler should then be able to grab the rod from the rod holder, pop the line from the release, and fight the fish. The release of the line shouldn't happen on its own. If it does, Engel says, you're missing fish. With the line tight to the release, you'll also see hits better.

Engel uses either Black's or Walker's adjustable downrigger release clips, and prefers Gamma 20- to 30-pound-test monofilament trolling line, a new copolymer, for his downrigger rods and reels. As for colors of salmon-trolling lures—spoons, flies, and crankbaits—he notes that fish preferences can change daily, sometimes hourly, but that chartreuse and green are always go-to colors for kings on Lake Michigan.

An interesting sidelight is that Engel no longer uses natural bait, either dead or alive, for trolling. He believes that while bait can still catch kings on certain days, artificial lures bring more fish to the net more consistently and with less hassle, mess, and expense. "For example, when the Mylar trolling fly came along years ago, it totally changed the entire concept of salmon trolling on the Great Lakes, particularly for kings," he says. "I use just one fly per leader on 40-pound-test Gamma fluorocarbon. I also put three or four colored beads in front of a fly, and I use a 1/0 Vanadium treble hook in the fly. I like a Howie fly in their 'green crinkle'

■ Downrigger weights can be either round or flat. If round, they're known as "cannonballs"; if flat, they're called "pancake weights." CHIP GROSS

■ Now that's a nice king! Charter captain Eric Schippa caught this Lake Michigan spring chinook trolling a Michigan Stinger spoon in a Natural Born Killer color pattern. CHIP GROSS

color. I've won nearly half a million dollars in salmon tournaments trolling a green crinkle Howie."

Engel has also discovered, as have most other serious anglers, that certain lures catch fish better than others. Not different lures, mind you, but lures of the exact same type, size, color, and manufacture. "Take a dozen new lures out of their packaging of the same color, size, and name brand, and two or three of those baits will outfish the others. It's not so much about color as it is just the right action or vibration. When I find such baits, they're like finding gold. I put them away and only tie them on again when fishing salmon tournaments, with money on the line."

Another secret that Engel has uncovered is the importance of trolling direction and the ability to read current. "In June and July, there are always strong currents in Lake Michigan, and if there's a secret to salmon trolling on big water, it's knowing how to read that current." He goes on to explain that current typically flows from south to north on Lake Michigan, but will sometimes reverse itself. "You can tell if you're not exactly in the middle of the current, because your trolling gear will be pulling off to one side of the boat. Sometimes wind will cause that to happen, too, so you have to know the difference, but you want to be trolling as straight into the current as possible. At times you can troll crosscurrent and be successful, but I normally catch two fish to one trolling directly into current as opposed to crosscurrent. During summer, I

want to be trolling straight into the strongest current I can find. Don't ask me why it works—I don't know. It just does."

In August, Engel begins trolling more plugs than spoons or flies, specifically J-plug-style lures, such as the Pedro Plug. "First thing in the morning, while it's still dark, glow plugs work very well," he says. "Charge 'em up with a small flash unit, put one on each line, and at the first crack of daylight, you'll likely have a fish fighting on every line."

Engel has found that during late summer, salmon usually bite like crazy for that first hour of daylight, but once the sun is up, it's time to take the glow lures off and put them away—far away. "The biggest tip I can give fishermen about glow plugs is to not leave them out in the sun, as constant exposure to light will wash them out. Any glow will burn out with too much sun exposure, and it also fades the colors of the bait. Those plugs catch fish much better if you don't leave them out in the sun all day once you're done fishing with them."

It is these kinds of details and on-the-water experience that have made Dave Engel the successful charter captain and tournament salmon fisherman he is. He sums it up this way: "As far as general techniques go, I'm not doing anything different than any other charter captain on the lake. But what I am doing are many small things differently—in other words, attention to detail. For instance, I'm a stickler about the little things that often make the difference between whether you catch fish or not—things such as the downrigger releases I use, the fluorocarbon leaders, the Vanadium treble hooks, on and on. . . . All those little details add up to big advantages—and more fish in the boat."

A final tip that Engel offers for searching for salmon on big water is to cooperate with other anglers, sharing fishing information. "Networking with other fishermen is extremely important for staying on fish. In fact, it's a must. There's a lot of water out there on the Great Lakes, and if you have no idea where to begin, you can waste an entire day fishing the wrong location. Sometimes making a move of only a few miles can make all the difference. But if you don't know those fish are there in the first place, you're stuck."

The networking concept also applies to Engel's tournament fishing. "If there's a captain that consistently finishes in the top five or ten boats of tournaments, you know he's working with other captains exchanging information," he says. "I know because I do it, and it's made me a lot of money."

Captain Russ Clark

Captain Russ Clark of Sea Hawk Charters has some additional thoughts on trolling the Great Lakes for salmon and steelhead. He's been a fishing guide on the lakes some twenty-five years, fishing year-round. He trolls southern Lake Michigan from the first week of April through mid-September for salmon and trout, then switches to steelhead the remainder of September through March in the St. Joseph River.

Like Dave Engel, Clark has watched the salmon and trout fisheries on Lake Michigan go through many changes, but he says that in recent years the fishing has been exceptional: "In the 1970s, when the salmon fishery was first getting started, we did catch more large fish. Today there are not as many big fish as there used to be, mainly because of a drop in baitfish numbers. But the fishery in general is very healthy. We have tremendous sportfishing on Lake Michigan."

For trolling Lake Michigan, Clark uses equipment similar to other Great Lakes charter captains: downriggers, directional divers, planer boards, and copper line. But he has not given up on lead-core line, as some captains have. He runs two and three colors of lead-core up high (taking lures 10 to 15 feet down), and copper line down low (getting lures 70 to 80 feet down).

"When fishing the Great Lakes, you really need a mixed arsenal of equipment that will take your lures to various depths," he explains. "I've found that running a combination of lead-core lines and copper lines allows me to get lures to all levels, shallow and deep." Clark may run as many as four lead-core lines per side of the boat (eight total), plus downrigger and diver rods.

A helpful hint that Clark has for trollers is to use line-counter reels with a high gear ratio, at least 4:1, because "they help get lines in quicker, as lines can be a long way out sometimes, possibly the length of a football field or more." He uses Okuma rods and reels, saying, "I like Okuma 10-foot rods for my directional divers, because the rods are limber and very forgiving."

Clark mainly uses spoons for lures, but will also troll crankbaits and occasionally live bait at times. He also places elastic snubbers, about a foot in length, behind his divers before tying on a leader. The snubbers help absorb the violent strike of a salmon or trout.

In addition, Clark uses a technique he's perfected that, at times, allows him to catch more than one fish at a time on the same line. On his downrigger rods, he attaches a "free-slider" to the main line, a lure that slides down to the natural bow in the trolling line, about halfway to the main lure.

"You're never quite sure at what depth the free-slider is running," says Clark. "But it helps by acting as an added attrac-

■ A client aboard charter captain Russ Clark's *Sea Hawk* battles a Lake Michigan salmon. Videotaping the action is Mark Romanack, best known for his *Precision Trolling* books (see sidebar on page 72-73). CHIP GROSS

tor for salmon. And the slider has a hook attached, so will catch fish. Many times I've caught two salmon at once using this setup, one on the main lure and another on the free-slider."

Southern Lake Michigan doesn't have much natural structure, so salmon and steelhead anglers look for temperature differences in the water to find offshore fish. "Only a degree or two of change in water temp can make all the difference," notes Clark. "And because there is so little structure, fish will relate to schools of baitfish, suspending below them."

Water temperature is also a key to finding early-season trout and salmon close to shore in the Great Lakes. In spring, the warmest water is usually closest to shore, making shorelines good places to begin looking for fish. Troll sandbars and any other near-shore structure you can find in water as shallow as 6 to 8 feet. Vary your trolling speed from 2 to 5 miles per hour, and use a zigzag pattern. In fall, kings and steelhead stage near river mouths, so fishing near pier heads can often be productive. Mid-September is usually the peak of the fall

salmon run. Water with a change in color can also hold salmon and trout, such as at river mouths where clouded water mixes with the clearer waters of the lake.

The right lure or bait presented at just the right depth and just the right trolling speed are all necessary to catch salmon and steelhead when fishing the Great Lakes. Additionally, to be successful, anglers must learn to spread their lines horizontally as well as vertically in the water column. Accomplishing all of this takes a dizzying array of fishing equipment: lead-core line, copper line, stainless-steel wire line, downriggers, directional divers, side planers, line-counter reels, and on and on.

The various fishing techniques associated with all that equipment are not mastered in just one fishing season—far from it. It may take a lifetime of fishing to become a top-notch salmon troller. But that's what keeps trollers coming back to the Five Sisters: the challenge of learning new and better ways to catch salmon and trout. The other half of the equation that brings us back is the promise of big fish and plenty of them. And quite possibly the salmon or steelhead of a lifetime . . .

CHAPTER EIGHT

Trolling for Pacific Northwest Salmon

Keith Jackson

Veteran outdoors writer Keith Jackson, a native of Washington State, has covered the sportfishing industry for more than twenty-five years. An expert in the tactics and techniques used for salmon and steelhead in the Pacific Northwest and Alaska, Jackson explains the various species of fish that most anglers in the region are pursuing: "The sport fish of most interest in the Pacific Northwest are chinook and coho salmon, followed by steelhead. Unfortunately, in Washington and Oregon, we have restricted runs of these species, as some thirty or more races of trout and salmon are on the endangered species list. That reduces much of the fishing activity in many of the traditional locations where stocks of fish mix."

Jackson goes on to say that while kings, coho, and steelhead see the most fishing effort, the Pacific Northwest also has good runs of pink salmon every other year. "In odd years the runs happen in Washington and Oregon, and in even years in upper British Columbia and Alaska."

Chum salmon, which are sometimes called "dog salmon," are also fished occasionally, but neither pinks nor chums are considered prime table fare by most people. Chum salmon have a very pale-colored meat. Compared to chinooks and cohos, whose meat is pink to reddish, locals consider chum salmon less desirable. However, as chinook and coho fishing seasons become more restricted, fishing pressure is increasing for pink and chum salmon.

According to Jackson, chinooks and cohos, as well as some chum salmon, are stocked by state fish and game agencies in the Pacific Northwest. "Although there hasn't been a lot of emphasis on catching chums for sport, they are very strong fighters when hooked. In fact, at one time it was the only fish a certain rod manufacturer would not guarantee its rods for. It's not that the rods weren't strong, it's just that chum salmon were stronger."

As for chum fishing techniques, Jackson says that "chums in the ocean approaching coastal rivers to spawn turn on to bait [herring, sardines, or prawn chunks] in a big way. The latest 'hot' technique is to fish a plug-cut herring under a float."

Chums change color quickly once they near their spawning rivers, "and start to

■ Outdoors writer Keith Jackson caught this king salmon off Montague Island near Seward, Alaska, mooching plug-cut herring. CHUCK SMOCK

look absolutely awful," according to Jackson. The males develop a strong kype—an extended lower jaw—with large, protruding teeth, and their body gets a lot of dark barring on the sides. Because of their appearance at spawning time, fishermen sometimes call chums "calico salmon."

Sockeye salmon don't get a lot of fishing pressure because they don't readily bite lures or bait, notes Jackson. "They're primarily plankton and krill feeders, and not extremely aggressive. However, when they move into Lake Washington, a large lake in the middle of Seattle, they bite fairly well on—believe it or not—bare black or red hooks pulled behind a flasher."

Jackson says that, in general, three types of fishing techniques dominate for salmon in the Pacific Northwest: trolling, jigging, and bait fishing, also known as "mooching." Trolling is generally done with downriggers, pulling either spoons or flies behind rotators or dodgers—similar to the methods used in the Great Lakes. Jigging is with heavy metal jigs or spoons, fished vertically. For mooching, anglers normally use herring as bait, either fresh or frozen, but sometimes sardines or candlefish.

In Alaska, most anglers pursue king salmon, with cohos being second in popularity. "At times, it's almost stupid, the fishing's so good in Alaska," says Jackson. Frequently, charter skippers anchor their boat in a salmon migration path and fish (mooch) with bait. The captains outfit their clients with a mooching sinker (a crescent-shaped weight with swivels at both ends), followed by a leader with two hooks and herring for bait. Anglers let their line out in the strong currents, and salmon swimming by attack the herring.

"If you're in the right place at the right time, such as near Sitka, you can often have all the kings you want in an hour," continues Jackson. Cohos, also known in Alaska as "silver salmon," are traditionally caught by skippers trolling either herring or artificial lures such as spoons or flies behind a flasher.

According to Jackson, river fishing for salmon and steelhead in Alaska and the Pacific Northwest is a completely different ball game than fishing for them in salt water. "It's almost like the fish become a completely different species once they enter the rivers."

Jackson stresses that because the Pacific Northwest and Alaska are such vast areas, many different fishing techniques and tactics have been developed for catching salmon and steelhead, all of which are effective at given times and places. "It's a big, big, big, fishery," Jackson concludes, "and no one knows it all."

Tom Nelson

Someone who may not know it all—but who knows plenty—is former charter captain Tom Nelson, founder of Salmon University. Originally from Seattle, Nelson now lives and fishes on Washington's

■ Dipsy Divers are a great way to get spoons down to depth when trolling, especially if salmon aren't too deep. Spring is a good time to use Dipsies, as water temperatures are relatively uniform from top to bottom and fish are usually high in the water column. CHIP GROSS

Kitsap Peninsula. He also fishes the coast of Washington State and British Columbia and has made several trips to Alaska.

"Salmon University, the Web site, has been around for five years or so, but I've been teaching salmon-fishing classes for twenty-five years at community colleges, continuing education programs, and sport shows up and down the West Coast," says Nelson. "I've had more than 6,000 people go through the classes."

Nelson fishes from a 24-foot North River Offshore aluminum boat, a big-

water craft. "It's probably bigger than most people would need for fishing Puget Sound, but because of its size, it can handle all types of water," he explains. "Puget Sound is very protected, and while it can get rough—even dangerous on occasion—it's not the type of water you see out on the open ocean."

But Nelson admits that Puget Sound is still serious water, the sound itself measuring about 120 miles long and up to 700 feet deep. "The majority of sportfishing takes place anywhere from 70 to 150 feet deep, so there is a lot of water to cover while looking for fish."

Nelson fishes for all five species of Pacific Northwest salmon. He chases chinook the majority of the year, coho in the fall, and pinks (also known as "humpies") every other year, as well as chum salmon and sockeye. "The best fishing for sockeye is in Lake Washington, right in front of Seattle," he adds.

The chinook is the most popular salmon with Nelson, simply because kings grow bigger than the other four species.

Chinooks have been reported as large as 100 pounds, but most of the fish in Puget Sound are 30 pounds or less. Nelson catches them year-round; however, a unique chinook fishery has developed during the winter. "We call them 'blackmouth,'" he says. "They're hatchery-raised fish that are delay-released. By holding them in pens in Puget Sound and delaying their release until later in the year, the fish don't migrate to the ocean as wild chinook do. Instead, they stay primarily in Puget Sound and along the coast of British

■ Downriggers, another way to take lures down in the water column, are used by salmon trollers in the Pacific Northwest, Alaska, and the Great Lakes.
CHIP GROSS

Columbia. The delayed-release program has created a wintertime salmon fishery where none existed previously."

To catch winter blackmouth chinook, Nelson fishes the bottom 10 to 20 feet of the water column. "The first thing you have to understand about blackmouth is that they are bottom feeders—they stay down deep," he explains. "Much of that behavior is just the nature of the fish, but it's also because the baitfish they feed on in winter are deep." Nelson either trolls for blackmouth using downriggers (he prefers Scotty) or mooches by drifting herring but, he says, "either way, keeping a bait or lure in the bottom 10 to 20 feet of water is critical."

If using downriggers, Nelson has this advice when choosing rods: "When buying a rod to use in conjunction with a downrigger, you've got to have a rod that will take a beating and still survive. In other words, putting your $300 graphite rod on a downrigger is not a good idea. You don't need sensitivity in a rod when fishing downriggers. When a fish hits and the line pops out of the downrigger release clip, you'll see it—you don't have to feel it."

Nelson uses Shimano Convergence and Talora series rods, but his favorite rod for trolling is a Lamiglas model XCF903, a combination rod made of graphite and fiberglass. The graphite gives the rod strength in the butt section, while the fiberglass makes it tough, able to withstand the wear and tear of downrigger

fishing. He matches his trolling rods with Shimano Tekota reels, models 300, 500, or 600. He's found that, like a dependable rod, Shimano reels are able to take a beating and still perform well in saltwater conditions.

Some of Nelson's reels are line-counters, for two reasons: "If you're mooching and you catch a fish, you can put the bait right back to the exact same depth with a line-counter reel. But a more fun application with big chinook and a line-counter is to watch how much line the fish peels off when it runs. When manufacturers first came out with line-counter reels years ago, I thought I didn't need them. But they've turned out to be a lot of fun. You can compare which salmon ran the farthest. Line-counters also come in handy if someone on board is not familiar with downrigger fishing and doesn't know exactly how far to let a line out behind a 'rigger."

For trolling line, Nelson prefers Gamma monofilament. He uses 20-pound test in winter and 25-pound test in summer, when bigger chinook are around. Big fish or small, Gamma has performed well for him. He and his friends have landed chinook over 50 pounds on both 20- and 25-pound-test line.

Nelson's basic trolling setup for chinook salmon is a flasher and plastic squid, or flasher and hoochie fished off a downrigger. If you're not familiar with the term *hoochie*, it's simply a piece of plastic that looks like a small group of baitfish when trolled through the water.

Another lure that Nelson uses frequently is a trolling fly. "During the past two years, I've been fortunate to get a few prototypes of the new Ace Hi trolling flies by Silver Horde," he notes. "They've turned out to be dynamite lures for chinook in our area. We also troll a lot of spoons, pulling those behind a flasher, too."

Nelson fishes mainly Silver Horde spoons, preferring three sizes: Coho Killer (small), #3 Kingfisher (medium), and Sonic Edge (large). As for color, his favorite is green glow in various design patterns. He also says that he's been catching good numbers of salmon recently on spoons with a UV coating, a new product from Silver Horde, noting that "salmon can see three colors of ultraviolet light that we can't."

Regarding leader material, Nelson doesn't believe that fluorocarbon is absolutely necessary in his fishing area, simply because there is so much plankton in the water that fish aren't seeing much of the line anyway. When fishing a flasher and fly or a flasher and hoochie, he ties his leaders four times the length of the flasher in summer, three times the length of the flasher in winter. Spoons, he believes, will work with either length leader. When trolling bait, such as herring, Nelson trails the bait 50 to 60 inches behind the flasher.

He likes a very stiff leader when trolling hoochies or flies, because those particular baits have no action of their own. A stiffer leader tends to toss a lure around more than a limp one. During his salmon seminars, Nelson advises students to use at least 40-pound-test leaders when fishing hoochies or flies, preferably as much as 60-pound test. For spoons, which provide their own action, lighter leaders can be used, 20- to 25-pound test.

Nelson goes on to say that what flashers do for a trolling setup is give added movement and sound to a lure, "and the more sound we create—as long as we are doing it in the right way—the more fish we seem to catch." He likes Pro-Troll flashers because they come equipped with electronic EChips. "EChips aren't magic, but we've found that they do add attraction to a lure. The electric pulse coming from the EChip seems to help fish zero in on a lure and not miss it as often."

To prove his point, Nelson mentions some underwater fishing photography that he did with a company a few years back: "In looking at that videotape, we were surprised to see how many salmon miss a lure when they first go to strike it. And they may not miss just once or twice, but sometimes as many as four or five times before they either get hooked or lose interest and swim off. With an EChip near a lure, the fish seem to sense that small amount of electricity. I believe it helps them better home in on a bait."

At first, Nelson was skeptical of E Chips—just another fishing gimmick, he thought—but became a believer after a salmon-fishing trip to Port Hardy, British Columbia, just off the north tip of Vancouver Island. "If you're only catching a few fish per day, it's tough to tell if something new

■ **After chinook, coho are the most sought-after salmon species in the Pacific Northwest, Alaska, and the Great Lakes.** CHIP GROSS

really works or not," he says. "But at Port Hardy we were catching between 80 and 150 fish per day. Under those conditions, we really started to see that the trolling set-ups using EChips did catch more salmon."

Nelson is quick to add that EChips aren't magic: "There is no magic in fishing. It's mainly just learning to do a few simple things right and paying attention to detail. But staying open-minded to new technology—when it proves to work—helps put more fish in the boat."

In addition to trolling, Nelson also puts salmon in the boat by bait fishing, or mooching. "Mooching is essentially using a weight to take your bait down to depth vertically," he says. "And unlike trolling, the boat's motor is shut off. Moochers are drifting with the current or tide."

The bait Nelson uses when mooching for chinook is usually plug-cut herring. The herring's head is cut off at an angle and the fish's entrails removed. The herring is also brined so that it's tougher, thus remaining on the hook longer. The secret to bait fishing for chinook, according to Nelson, is to keep the herring on or near the bottom, bouncing bottom with the sinker.

Coho are the second-most popular salmon species with Nelson, and as with chinook, they are delayed-released by the state fish and game agency. "Fall produces quite a coho fishery in our area," notes Nelson. "We fish the entire water column for them, anywhere from the surface down to 150 feet deep. The difference is whether we're fishing for coho in the summer or winter."

Nelson trolls a little faster for coho than for chinook, and often begins fishing shallow first thing in the morning. He trolls for chinook at 2.5 miles per hour and for coho at 3.5 miles per hour. And there is another difference that he mentions about fishing for cohos versus kings: "With chinook, we're trolling drop-offs and underwater shelves along Puget Sound, Vancouver Island, or wherever else we're fishing. Chinook seem to be a more structure-oriented fish. But coho can be found anywhere, from right on shore to 5 miles out in the middle of Puget Sound. With coho you just have to hunt for them more, but once you find them, they're fairly easy to catch."

CHAPTER NINE

Trolling for Trophy Chinooks from Small Boats

Outdoors writer and communicator John Beath began salmon fishing at the age of eight, catching his first chinook salmon—23 pounds—from Washington's Puget Sound. "From that time on I've been completely hooked on salmon fishing," Beath says. "When I was growing up, my parents didn't own a boat, so we fished mainly from piers and jetties. One summer I remember catching fifty-four salmon from a single pier."

Beath's passion for fishing continued to grow as he did. At one point in his life he worked for Rivers Inlet Resort, teaching guests how to fish. The resort, located on the northeast tip of Vancouver Island, just off the central coast of British Columbia, is a true wilderness fishing camp, accessible only by floatplane or boat. Beath has fished the area some eighteen years, taking fourteen chinook salmon over 50 pounds, two of which were over 60 pounds. He also once lost a salmon that he estimates could have topped 70 pounds. Beath holds the International Game Fish Association (IGFA) record in the 6-pound-test line category for chinook salmon (51 pounds, 4 ounces), caught August 18, 2004, near Rivers Inlet.

"The area around Rivers Inlet is definitely a trophy fishery, but it's also a difficult area to fish," says Beath. "You have to be precise with your technique and trolling depth."

The technique he uses is slow-trolling herring, either whole or cut-plug. "Cut-plug" simply means that the head and entrails of the herring have been removed. If whole herring is used as bait, the fish measure from 5 to 8 inches long. Beath also rigs the bait in such a way that it is slightly curved when hooked front and back. This causes the herring to corkscrew through the water when trolled. He also likes to squirt his own specially formulated Super Scent on the bait.

Beath uses a 20-pound-test monofilament main line with about a 5-foot, 20-pound-test leader of Stren fluorocarbon in the Coral Mist color. His hook setup at the end of the line includes two Mustad hooks (Model 92553S) in either a 3/0, 4/0, or 5/0 combination, with the smaller of the two hooks tied on the end of the rig. If you don't want to take the time to tie your own hooks and leaders, a Luhr Jensen Herring 101 Rig provides a similar setup.

John Beath holds the International Game Fish Association (IGFA) record in the 6-pound-test line category for chinook salmon. COURTESY JOHN BEATH

"I like those particular Mustad hooks, because you can sharpen them like a knife blade and they keep their sharpness," Beath says. "And when I'm trolling, I want a hook with a straight tip, not one that curves in toward the shank. I believe that a straight hook produces more hookups. Mustad hooks are so tough and of such quality that at the fishing resort we resharpened and reused them for two or three years. Some of my personal hooks are five or six years old, and I'm still using them."

Beath catches trophy chinooks by trolling very slowly, 0.8 to 1.2 miles per hour, just barely keeping the bait moving. He trolls from relatively small boats, 14- to 18-foot fiberglass Livingstons with an open cockpit. Beath has successfully used this slow-troll tactic for big kings throughout all of Washington, Oregon, British Columbia, and much of Alaska. "About the only changes you'll see throughout the region are the kinds of rods and reels used and the amount of weight on the line," he notes. "In some deep areas, downriggers are used to take the bait down to depth."

Instead of downriggers, Beath prefers a round, 6- to 8-ounce weight. The weight attaches to the line on something known as a "slide-O," which slides up and down the main line. He does not use line-counter reels; instead, he measures the amount of line he lets out in "pulls." A pull is roughly an arm's length of line. Each person's arm length is slightly different, but the idea is to be able to replicate the distance should you catch a fish at a certain depth. To make a more accurate depth presentation, Beath first measures out 20 feet of line with a measuring tape, then marks that point on his line with a black permanent marker.

"At Rivers Inlet we don't normally have to get our baits below 20 feet, because the salmon are lying just under a layer of glacial water near the surface," he says. "I let line out until my mark is at the surface. That way I know exactly how deep my bait is trolling. It's a very precise method of fishing."

Beath uses Canadian-style G. Loomis mooching rods (10½ feet, model GL2 STR1201S), preferring them because of their sensitivity. "It's a medium-action rod, but stout enough to handle at least 8 ounces of lead plus a big salmon." He matches the rods with single-action Islander reels, in his opinion the best-quality single-action reel on the market. He also sets his reel drags extremely loose.

For anglers who don't particularly like single-action reels, Beath recommends line-counter reels. He says they make a big difference when trying to maintain precise depth control in places like Tillamook Bay or the Nehalem River mouth, both of which provide top-notch chinook fishing in Oregon.

"When fishing in British Columbia, you can legally run as many lines as you wish as long as everyone on board a boat has a fishing license," notes Beath. "When I'm fishing by myself, I like to run six trolling lines—two on each side of the

■ Trolling from small boats off river mouths during early fall is a great way to catch fall kings in the Great Lakes, as the fish are staging for their annual spawning run up the rivers. CHIP GROSS

boat and two off the front—placing all the rods in rod holders." He believes that you won't hook as many fish if you try hand-holding a rod: "It's not only tiring with all that weight on the end, but when you feel a bite, most people tend to react too quickly and pull the bait away from the fish. Big chinooks need a little time to get themselves well hooked."

A trick that Beath uses on sunny days is to troll what he calls the "shadow line," that line on the water where sunlight and shadow meet. By placing his boat right on this line, half his baits are running in

shadow and half in sunlight. He's found that big kings will often hang out along this line, charging out from the shadows to grab a bait flashing by in the sunlight.

Regional anglers who fish the open ocean off the west coast of Vancouver Island concentrate on deeper waters, anywhere from 90 to more than 200 feet down. Using downriggers, they place their baits near the bottom around structure, such as a bank or underwater reef. One of the chinook's favorite foods while in the ocean is candlefish. These slim, ribbonlike fish spawn in bottom sands, and during that time salmon can be found on or near the bottom, feeding on them.

"You can tell when salmon are feeding on candlefish, because you'll see scrapes on their gill plates from them being right down on the bottom," says Beath. "When that happens, we can catch them by jigging as well as trolling."

When jigging deep water, Beath uses Point Wilson Dart Jigs, varying the weight of the jig with the depth of the water. When trolling deep, open water he uses a variety of baits: Silver Horde or Tomic plugs, flashers and flies, flashers and squid, or flashers and herring. Spoons have also become popular and are very productive throughout the West Coast region.

"Trolling spoons is a very effective method for catching chinook," remarks Beath. "I like a Coyote spoon anywhere from 42 to 56 inches behind a flasher, the length depending upon the mood of the fish on any particular day and how fast I'm trolling."

Off the east coast of Vancouver Island, between the island and the mainland of British Columbia, shore anglers mainly fish points of land, where currents move water around the points. "And we're always trying to locate baitfish near the points," Beath notes, "because where you find baitfish, you'll also find salmon."

He adds that good bank fishing for both salmon and steelhead can be had not only from Vancouver Island, but throughout the Pacific Northwest. "There's lots

BINOCULARS AND OTHER ESSENTIAL FISHING GEAR

Fishing guide John Beath suggests carrying a pair of binoculars on board whenever trolling, for several reasons: "If you're not getting bit, it allows you to watch other nearby anglers and see what they're doing. For instance, in the area I fish, I can tell how deep other fishermen are running their baits by watching how many 'pulls' of line they let out. I can also see what size lead weight they are using to take their baits down and if that lead is colored or not. I can also tell about how fast they are trolling by the angle their trolling lines enter the water."

In addition to having binoculars on board, Beath likes to keep in contact with other boats in his fishing party by using inexpensive walkie-talkie-type radios. He also always has a VHF radio on board with scan capabilities, noting, "It not only increases safety while on the water, but you'll sometimes hear of a hot bite in another area that you can take advantage of."

of access along the coast from Oregon, throughout Washington, and into British Columbia. As you get more into British Columbia, you see more dink-float fishing from shore, anglers using 10- to 12-foot rods to suspend a jig or bait at a precise level above the bottom. They watch the

■ **Chinooks love trolling flies—especially green in color—but flies must be trolled behind either a dodger or flasher to give the lure action.** CHIP GROSS

float for a strike, then set the hook. The technique is really just now starting to catch on not only in BC, but in Washington and Oregon, too."

But Beath, like many anglers, still prefers to drift bait along the bottoms of rivers without a float, using what he calls a "slinky" weight to take the bait down. A slinky is made from a small section of parachute cord filled with lead shot. These weights—either commercially made or homemade—slide between rocks better than a solid lead weight, lessening the number of snags. Also, using solid lead weights can make for a somewhat loud presentation, as the lead is constantly banging off rocks as it works its way downstream. A slinky weight dampens the sound, or vibration, your hands feel through the rod, making it easier to recognize subtle bites.

A final tip that John Beath has for bait fishermen is to use whole-cooked shrimp, purchased from a grocery store or seafood market. He prefers the shrimp small, about sixty to eighty per pound, and takes about a dozen along on each fishing trip, peeling them before putting them on the hook.

"I put the small end of the shrimp tail through an egg loop above the hook eye—that way the bait corkscrews through the water when it's drifted or retrieved," explains Beath. "Shrimp are very oily and leave a lot of scent in the water. It's the most underused, overlooked bait in the Northwest, probably because most people just don't know about it. I've caught more steelhead using whole-cooked shrimp than I have on salmon eggs or sand shrimp combined."

CHAPTER TEN

Fishing Alaska for Salmon and Steelhead

John Yeager

"Fishing has always been a big part of my life," says John Yeager, charter captain and fishing guide from Wrangell, Alaska. "I grew up in the Midwest, and bought my first johnboat and electric motor at age twelve. I would hitch the boat to my parents' lawn tractor and tow it down the road to a local quarry pond and fish for bass and bluegills."

Yeager has since graduated a bit in his fishing. After a seventeen-year career in the U.S. Coast Guard, he now charters for king and coho salmon, as well as other saltwater species, along Alaska's southeast coast.

He begins his charter-fishing season in early May, normally fishing through the end of August. The peak season for kings out of Wrangell is mid-May to mid-June, with the possibility of good fishing continuing for a few weeks thereafter. Cohos typically bite best in late July through August, maybe even to mid-September.

"Cohos feed heavily and pack on a lot of weight during that month-and-a-half to two-month period," says Yeager. "Early in the run you catch fish weighing 7 to 8 pounds. But by the end of the run, we're catching fish that may weigh 18 pounds. King salmon in our area average 28 to 30 pounds, measuring 33 to 35 inches. A big chinook will weigh 47 to 55 pounds. By contrast, Kenai River kings, in southwest Alaska, can weigh 60 to 70 pounds."

For catching king salmon, both trolling and mooching, Yeager uses Lamiglas rods (8 feet, 6 inches), the Certified Pro model in a medium to heavy action. He matches the rods with Abu-Garcia 7000 IC3 reels, filling them with Maxima Ultra-Green 40-pound-test monofilament line.

"That's my standard tackle setup, but I also like to have a second rod option for my clients," Yeager says. "For people who have not fished much for salmon in Alaska, I give them the heavier rod I just described. But for my more experienced fishermen, I'll hand them a two-piece Lamiglas MBC graphite rod with an Ambassador Record 60 reel and 25-pound-test line."

For trolling, Yeager ties his own slip-leaders, using Maxima 40-pound-test fluorocarbon. He likes red Gamakatsu 5/0 octopus hooks for the rig. The slip-rig is

■ Charter captain John Yeager of Wrangell, Alaska, holds a big king caught by one of his clients, Lynette McIntosh of Bishop, California. NANCY BAY

made up of two hooks, the end hook being tied stationary. The front hook is tied to slide up and down the leader.

"When I'm trolling a slip-rig, I use herring for bait," Yeager notes, "and rig it so that both hooks come out the same side of the fish. I also cut the tail off the herring, which creates the illusion of a wounded baitfish, as well as puts blood in the water. And I rig the herring so that there is a slight bend in the body of the fish. That gives it a very distinct roll through the water when trolled."

In relatively shallow water, he ties a banana weight into the line. A banana weight has a six-bead swivel on one end and a barrel swivel on the other. The leader ties to the six-bead end, with the main line tying to the swivel on the other end of the weight.

■ Captain John Yeager prepares herring for trolling by removing the tail and rigging both hooks to come out of the same side of the bait. JOHN YEAGER

Yeager's primary trolling method, especially in deeper water, is with downriggers. He uses three Scotty downriggers with 10-pound pancake weights, positioning one 'rigger on each side of the boat and one off the stern. He sets his baits to run 5 to 10 feet apart in depth, all the while watching his electronics for balls of baitfish. "The baitfish I'm looking for early in the season are needlefish, then herring later in the season," he says. "And I try and match the size of my baits to the size of baitfish salmon are eating. While cleaning fish, I always cut open a few salmon stomachs to see what's inside."

Yeager buys frozen herring that he soaks in a brine solution before using them as bait. He likes a medium-size herring for much of his trolling, 6 to 8 inches long before removing about an inch of tail. And if he can get them, he looks for larger-bodied herring, believing the bigger fish present a bigger target for salmon to see and strike.

To make the herring even more enticing, he injects his baits with Pro-Cure herring oil, noting, "Pro-Cure is an incredible salmon attractant. As the herring is trolled through the water, the oil seeps out, creating an oil slick of scent behind the bait. It's a fish attractant like no other I've ever used. . . . I'd highly recommend it."

Yeager normally trolls his baits anywhere from 35 to 45 feet deep, but has caught kings using his system as deep as 80 feet. He trolls for kings at a speed of 1.5 to 2.1 knots, or about 3 to 4 miles per hour. "My basic trolling approach is to look for balls of baitfish on my electronics, then troll through those balls with my baits anywhere from the middle of the school to the top. You don't ever want to troll below baitfish, as salmon tend to feed up, attacking baitfish schools from below. They shoot up from underneath, eat or wound whatever baitfish they can, then circle around and come back through the school again, picking up any stragglers."

If Yeager is not trolling bait, he's either pulling spoons or Silver Horde Ace Hi trolling flies behind Hot Spot flashers. "I like Ace Hi flies because they're a hard-headed fly, almost like a combination fly and hoochie," he says. He prefers Silver Horde and Gold Star spoons, 4 and 5 inches in length. For kings, he may occasionally even use up to a 7-inch spoon.

He replaces the original hooks on his spoons with either a 5/0 or 6/0 Siwash Gamakatsu hook, which is a long, straight-shank model. "The tip isn't offset, so I use a pair of pliers to hold the bend of the hook, then hold the shank in my hand and twist opposite to put a slight twist in the hook," says Yeager. "I've found it helps fish hook up better than leaving the hook straight."

Spoon colors Yeager likes range from solid gold, to gold and silver striped, to blues and greens. "Black spots seem to work well on all these colors, except gold for some reason," he notes. "Silver Horde and Gold Star both put an awe-

■ **A Hot Spot chrome dodger and Silver Horde Ace Hi trolling fly, a deadly combination for Alaskan kings.** JOHN YEAGER

some UV coating on their spoons that I like real well, too." He places spoons about 12 feet back in the downrigger clip before lowering them to depth, then trolls spoons a little faster than when fishing bait.

Yeager trolls the same Ace Hi flies and flashers for coho salmon as for kings, but in addition will add a small spoon or two to his spread. He's especially fond of Silver Horde's Coho Killer. He trolls a little faster for cohos than kings, 2.5 to 3 knots.

He also fishes lighter tackle for cohos, using the lighter of the two rod and reel setups described earlier.

For cohos, as with salmon, Yeager likes a UV coating on spoons, but believes that cohos like wilder colors and patterns than kings: pinks, oranges, chartreuse, and spoons with black spots. He clips coho spoons into his downriggers the same distance as for kings.

"The more aggressive the spoon action and color, the more cohos seem to like it," says Yeager. "And when a coho fights, it's not like the heavy pull of a king salmon. They're a totally different animal, running from side to side when hooked or charging the boat. If you try and troll too many lines when coho fishing, coho will tangle you up like crazy. But a few tangled lines are worth it, as coho are a lot of fun to fight and catch."

Yeager adds that cohos can occasionally be seen feeding on the surface. "That's when I hand my clients a medium-weight spinning rod with a spinner attached," he says. "A silver, orange, or pink Blue Fox spinner with a number 4 or 5 blade is deadly for cohos. When anchored while fishing for halibut with a main rod in a rod holder, you can be casting a second rod for cohos."

Yeager recently acquired a new boat for his Alaska charter-fishing service. He's now the proud owner of a custom-built, 35-foot aluminum boat by Svendsen Marine, boasting an 11½-foot beam. The boat is powered by twin 250-horse Mercury Verado four-stroke outboards and can accommodate up to six charter clients, plus Yeager and a first mate.

One final piece of advice that Yeager has about salmon trolling is to not be afraid to try different methods and techniques of fishing, some possibly unorthodox. "I kind of pride myself in taking different avenues from the norm. I'm constantly trying things that other fishermen won't. A lot of times things don't pan out, but sometimes they do," he says. "To become a better salmon fisherman, don't be afraid to constantly experiment."

Marlin Benedict

Longtime guide Marlin Benedict fishes for salmon in the freshwater rivers near Wrangell, Alaska—primarily with fly-fishing tackle. "I got started fly fishing in an odd way," says Benedict. "As a teenager, I found a box of artificial flies that another fisherman had inadvertently left on a rock along a stream. I took the box home, borrowed an old fly rod from a buddy, and taught myself to fly fish. Once I caught my first fish on a fly, I was hooked for life." He has since caught all five species of Alaskan salmon on a fly: chinook, coho, sockeye, pink, and chum.

Benedict transports his clients to freshwater streams in a 17-foot jet boat. He then beaches the craft and clients wade the river, fishing the various holes from shore. Benedict charters primarily for pink and chum salmon because, surprisingly, chinooks are not allowed to be specifically targeted by sport anglers fishing southeast Alaska rivers.

"The regulation has to do with a treaty agreement between the U.S. and Canada," he explains. "Once chinooks enter our streams, we cannot legally keep any if we catch them. But they hit the same baits and lures that pink and chum salmon do, so you're going to hook one from time to time."

Benedict's favorite salmon fly is actually a saltwater tarpon fly, known as a Charlie. "It's florescent hot pink in color. The body is weighted, which helps it get down in the strike zone more quickly, without having to add any lead shot to the line. And there's no hackle around the body of the fly, just a little marabou or a small piece of rabbit's fur for a tail."

Benedict uses a sinking-tip fly line on a 7- or 8-weight Cabela's PT rod. Streams in his area normally run only about 3 to 5 feet deep at the deepest, so a 5- to 6-foot leader is about right. For leader material, he uses Maxima Ultra-Green 8-pound-test monofilament, tying it directly from the fly line to the fly, no tippet.

For catching pinks and chums, Benedict advises his clients to position themselves above a hole, then cast quartering downstream. "Mend your cast as the line floats downstream and be ready, as many times a fish will hit at the very bottom of a swing. Keep a tight line, and you'll feel the fish hit. If you don't keep your line tight, a fish can pick up the fly and spit it out before you ever know you've had a bite."

He says that he has seen this happen many times. While wearing polarized sunglasses, especially in clear water, he's observed a salmon strike before his client even knew that a fish was close. "I'll be screaming at them to set the hook, and they won't have a clue why I'm yelling. The technique I described definitely requires a tight line and concentration to be successful."

Benedict also advises clients to keep their fly rod tip low, just above the water's surface. "You'll be able to feel every little bump on the end of the line if you do. I have clients who insist on holding their rod tip 2 feet above the water; that creates belly in the line and they don't feel the bites." He does not use a strike indicator when fly fishing, but does watch the connection where his main line ties to the leader. "If that knot takes a sudden dive, I'm setting the hook," he says.

Even though Benedict is in love with fly fishing, he also carries spinning gear in his boat, just in case the salmon aren't responding to flies on any particular day. With spinning gear (Shakespeare Ugly Stik rods and Shimano reels), he normally casts ⅛-ounce pink or purple jigs. Instead of suspending the jig beneath a float, he casts it directly into a pool and bounces it downstream with the current. "Think of the technique as working a corky and yarn rig along the bottom," he suggests. When fishing spinners with spinning tackle, Benedict likes pink Bang Tails, Rooster Tails, or Mepps inline spinners.

If clients prefer, he will also fish for steelhead in freshwater streams, but the fishing regulations in his region are very restrictive. Anglers are allowed to keep only two steelhead per year, and the fish must measure at least 36 inches. And although drifting bait is a common steel-

■ **Find an active school of steelhead while trolling, and catching doubles as well as triples is a real possibility. When it's right, it's right!** CHIP GROSS

heading technique throughout most of North America, surprisingly, it is illegal for steelhead fishing in southeast Alaska.

Benedict adjusts by catching steelhead on everything from artificial flies, to Hot Shot plugs, to jigs under a float, to drifting a corky and yarn. He likes orange corkies in combination with orange and pink yarn.

The past few years, he has spent more time fishing jigs under a float for steelhead, his favorite jig colors being pink, purple, and orange. "Float fishing is a great way for many of my clients to catch steelhead," he notes, "especially in rivers with a lot of potential snags, as the float helps keep the jig up off the bottom."

■ **Fishing guide Marlin Benedict shows off an April steelhead caught from a southeast Alaska river.** JAMES ROLLAND

For jig fishing, he ties a 2½- to 3-foot leader of 8-pound-test mono. In early April, before the snows melt, Alaskan rivers in the southeast section of the state run fairly clear. As a result, Benedict believes that fluorocarbon leaders might be helpful then, "but once the rains begin and the snow starts to melt, our rivers color up and become brackish. A lot of our streams also originate from glaciers, so can get milky. Most of the time, in my opinion, fluorocarbon leaders aren't necessary."

The best river steelheading in southeast Alaska takes place from the end of April to the middle of June, but some years steelhead can be caught as late as the Fourth of July. The average steelhead will weigh 8 to 10 pounds. A keeper fish of 36 inches can weigh 10 to 12 pounds or more.

In addition to guiding both anglers and hunters to Alaskan adventures, Benedict teaches fly-fishing classes, encouraging his students to keep things as simple as possible. "Fishing is not complicated," he says. "You simply want as little as possible on the end of your line that will allow you to catch fish." Marlin Benedict should know—he's caught a lot of them.

Vary the trolling-rod lengths in 1-foot increments to put separation between rods. Equipping the rods with identical reels decreases the chance for confusion as to how a reel works when a **fish hits.** CHIP GROSS

A Final Word . . .

If you've read this far, you're no doubt a serious steelheader or salmon fisherman—or soon will be. And if you apply the techniques described in *Pro Tactics: Steelhead & Salmon* and are persistent, you will catch fish—guaranteed. But once that steelhead or salmon is securely in the net, you have a decision to make: Do you keep the fish, or turn it loose to swim free and fight again another day for another angler?

Your first consideration should be the legalities. If steelhead/salmon are not legal to keep in your fishing area, or you've

■ **Leaving port, the promise of a new day on the water. What will the fishing hold . . .?** CHIP GROSS

caught one that's too small, there is no question that the fish should be released immediately. But if steelhead/salmon are legal to harvest in the waters you fish, don't let anyone make you feel guilty for keeping fish if you want to. Steelhead and salmon, as well as other game-fish species, are a renewable natural resource and a great source of nutritious food.

At the same time, if you are killing fish just to impress your fishing buddies, you might want to rethink your actions. For example, how many trophy fish hanging from the wall are too many? How many brag boards lined with fish at the dock are enough? Only you can answer that.

Just keep in mind that we enjoy tremendous fishing opportunities in North America that much of the world does not. And with those opportunities comes a certain responsibility—a responsibility we have as anglers to use wisely the fishery resources with which we've been blessed. After a lifetime of fishing, I've learned that conservation can mean both keeping a fish or letting it swim away. The final decision is yours. I'm sure you'll make the right choice . . .

—W. H. "Chip" Gross

Contacting the Pros

I would like to sincerely thank all the fishing guides, charter captains, outdoors writers, and others who made this book possible. During my lifetime I've found that anglers are some of the most friendly, helpful people I've ever met. In this book, those interviewed have unselfishly shared their vast knowledge of their part of the fishing world. Below are their names and contact information, should you want to ask them a specific question or possibly book a fishing trip. Thanks again, guys. And if we haven't already taken a trip together, I look forward to fishing with you.

—Chip Gross

John Beath
Outdoors Writer
www.halibut.net

Captain Marlin Benedict
Fish Wrangell Alaska
www.fishwrangell.com

Joe Cinelli
Cinelli's Niagara River Guides
www.niagarafishingguides.com

Captain Russ Clark
Sea Hawk Charters
www.fishseahawk.com

Captain Dave Engel
Best Chance Too Sportfishing Charters
www.bestchancetoo.com

Bob Hanko
Cranberry Creek Marina
www.cranberrycreekmarina.com

Keith Jackson
Outdoors Writer
ckjackson@olypen.com

Greg Kain
Kain's Fishing Adventures
www.kainsfishingadventures.com

Jeff Liskay
Silverfury Guide Service
(440) 781-7536

Tom Nelson
Salmon University
www.salmonuniversity.com

Mark Romanack
Outdoors Writer
www.precisionangling.com

Terry Wiest
Steelhead University
www.steelheaduniversity.com

Scott Stouder
Trout Unlimited
sstouder@tu.org

Captain John Yeager
Timber Wolf Charters
www.timberwolfcharters.com

INDEX

About the Author

Freelance writer, photographer, speaker, and editor W. H. "Chip" Gross has been fascinated by the out-of-doors all his life. At an early age Gross was taught to fish by his maternal grandfather, and as a young teenager learned to hunt from his father. Those two activities eventually led him to many other outdoors pursuits, such as birding, canoeing, and camping, to name just a few.

Today, much of Gross's writing revolves around sportfishing. He is a senior writer for *Fishing Tackle Retailer* magazine, a columnist for *Great Lakes Angler* magazine, and outdoors editor for *Country Living* magazine. He holds a four-year degree in wildlife management from Ohio State University and completed a twenty-seven-year career with the Ohio DNR, Division of Wildlife, in 2002.

Gross is the author of two previous books, *Ohio Wildlife Viewing Guide* (part of the Falcon Publishing Wildlife Viewing Series) and the outdoors novel *Home, at Last, Is the Hunter*, WORDsmith Publishing. He lives with his wife, Jan, near Fredericktown, Ohio. You can contact Chip through www.chipgross.com.